The
Cockatiel
Handbook

Mary Gorman

BARRON'S

About the Author

A chance encounter with a 10-week-old cockatiel was all it took to launch Mary Gorman on raising exotic birds as a hobby. Twelve years later, she has written for a wide variety of pet bird magazines in both the U.S. and U.K., as well as books on lovebirds and caiques for Barron's Educational Series. A former animal caregiver with the Dakin Pioneer Valley Humane Society, Mary currently lives in Western Massachusetts with her family, three extremely well behaved cats and a small assortment of birds, including the cockatiel who started it all.

Acknowledgements

The author wishes to thank Colleen Ranger of Western Australia for the information on wild cockatiels; Beth Gorman and Ruth Wolpin for their help with translations; registered dietitian Kathy Gorman for the nutritional information provided; Heather Smith of Dave's Pet City for introducing me to Cookie and guiding me through my early days as a cockatiel owner; Emily Kolod and the staff of the Western New England Animal Care and Adoption Center; and the Dakin Pioneer Valley Humane Society for both the work that they do and their assistance with this book.

Dedication

For my daughter, Katie Fox, who was "into" birds long before I was. I love you, Honey.

Photo Credits

Joan Balzarini: pages 4, 26, 30, 31, 46 (right), 48 (bottom), 50 (top), 51 (top and bottom), 53, 56, 70, 72, 89 (top), 93, 102, 108, 128, 133, 136 (top); Paulette Johnson: pages 6, 7, 16, 18, 35, 49, 61, 68, 84, 87, 92 (bottom), 97, 98, 111, 118; B. Everett Webb: pages 2, 8, 9, 12, 14, 15, 20, 22, 25, 33, 36, 38, 39, 40, 43, 44, 45, 46 (left), 47, 48 (top), 50 (bottom), 52, 57, 58, 62, 64, 69, 76, 79, 80, 83, 89 (bottom), 90, 92 (top), 100, 105, 107, 110, 112, 116, 120, 123, 124, 127, 131, 134, 135, 136 (bottom).

Cover Photos

Joan Balzarini: back cover; Shutterstock: front cover; B. Everett Webb: front cover (bottom right), inside front cover, inside back cover.

All inquiries should be addressed to:
Barron's Educational Series, Inc.
250 Wireless Boulevard
Hauppauge, New York 11788
www.barronseduc.com

ISBN-13: 978-0-7641-4292-5
ISBN-10: 0-7641-4292-5

Library of Congress Catalog Card No. 2009019164

Library of Congress Cataloging-in-Publication Data
Gorman, Mary.
    The cockatiel handbook / Mary Gorman.
        p.   cm.
    Includes bibliographical references and index.
    ISBN-13: 978-0-7641-4292-5
    ISBN-10: 0-7641-4292-5
    1. Cockatiel. I. Title.
SF473.C6G67   2009
636.6′8656—dc22   2009019164

Printed in China

9 8 7 6

Important Note
The information contained in this book is as accurate and up-to-date as possible at the time of publication, however it is not intended as a substitute for professional, medical advice. In the event of illness or accident, please take your cockatiel to a qualified veterinary professional as soon as possible.

Contents

1. Introduction   1
    Thc Wild Cockatiel   1
    A Brief History of the Cockatiel   2

2. Is a Cockatiel Right for You?   5
    Pet Potential   5
    Will It Talk?   9
    Cockatiels and Kids   9
    Cockatiels and Other Pets   11

3. Are You Right for a Cockatiel?   13
    Cost   13
    Space   14
    Time   14
    Other Considerations   15

4. Getting Ready   19
    Cage   19
    Play Stands   23
    Perches   24
    Cuttlebones and Mineral Blocks   27
    Other Supplies   28
    Veterinary Care   34
    Things You Don't Need   35

5. Choosing Your Cockatiel   37
    What to Look For   37
    Where to Find Your Bird   38
    Making Your Selection   41
    Mutations   45
    Signs of an Unhealthy Bird   52

6.	**Bringing Your Cockatiel Home**	**55**
	Quarantine	55
	Cage Location	55
	Making Introductions	56
	Handling Your Cockatiel	59
	Interacting with Your Bird	60
7.	**Cockatiel Care and Maintenance**	**63**
	Basic Care	63
	Taming, Training, and Tricks	69
8.	**Behavior**	**77**
	Bad Behaviors	77
	Reading Cockatiel Body Language	88
9.	**Diet and Nutrition**	**94**
	Comfort Foods	94
	Staple Foods	94
	Vegetables and Fruits	97
	Mixing It Up	99
	Foods to Avoid	102
10.	**Safety**	**103**
	Wing Trimming	103
	Lost Birds	103
	Cockatiel Hazards	106
	How to Medicate Your Cockatiel	112
11.	**Health**	**115**
	Is Your Cockatiel Ill?	115
	Common Cockatiel Ailments	117
	Emergency First Aid for Cockatiels	120
12.	**Egg, Chick, Cockatiel**	**126**
	To Breed or Not to Breed?	126
	The Mating Mood	127
	Eggs	129
	Chicks	132
	Resources	**137**
	Index	**138**

Chapter One
Introduction

I met my first cockatiel in June of 1997. While I was visiting a pet store, a ten-week-old gray cockatiel caught my attention. He rushed to the front of the cage when I stopped to look, chirping excitedly as he pressed his head against the bars to get me to scratch it for him. When I walked away, he followed as far as the confines of the cage would let him, and then called and called after me as I left. On my way back out of the store, he shrieked with joy to see me again and paced the front of the cage hurriedly, trying to get my attention.

I asked the clerk if he was tame, and she opened the cage door. Even though his wings were clipped, he barreled out of the cage, launching himself at me. He clung to the front of my shirt as if his feet were Velcro. He ignored the clerk and the other shoppers who stopped to admire him. I got the impression that I was the only one he wanted. I ended up taking him home, of course. I had picked out many pets over the years, but this was the first time a pet had ever picked *me*!

Cockatiels are like that—friendly, curious, and alert. They are almost unfailingly cheerful and truly seem to *enjoy* being with people. Their forgiving nature and ease of care make them the second-most-popular pet bird in the English-speaking world, and they make an excellent starter bird for someone who has no prior bird-owning experience.

The Wild Cockatiel

Cockatiels are native to Australia, living in open areas near bodies of water in the arid and semi-arid parts of the country, but avoiding the more humid northern, eastern, and southern coastal areas. They like to perch on the topmost branches of dead trees, where their gray coloring acts as camouflage against the branch, making them difficult to spot. Wild cockatiels usually live in pairs or small flocks. They may band together to form large flocks near a body of water or farms, where they are considered a pest because they cause considerable damage to grain crops.

Wild cockatiels are very common in Australia, in part because they are prolific breeders. Cockatiels may

start to breed before they reach their first birthday, and typically lay four to five eggs in each clutch. The young start to leave the nest at about five weeks old, and the parents may produce multiple clutches each year.

Unlike pet cockatiels, which have been bred to exhibit a variety of color and feather patterns, wild cockatiels are primarily gray birds, with white edges on the wings and tail, a crest of tall, narrow feathers on the top of the head, and a round reddish-orange spot of either side of the face. Adult males have bright yellow faces, while females and young birds' faces are primarily gray with muted yellow. Adult cockatiels are about 12½ inches (32 cm) long.

Cockatiels' closest relatives are cockatoos, another genus of Aus-tralian parrots. Cockatiels are the smallest members of the cockatoo family, but unlike cockatoos, they have thinner bodies and long tails. Cockatiels' legs are also further back on their bodies, so they are not able to use their feet like hands to manipulate objects or to hold their food while they are eating.

A Brief History of the Cockatiel

The first Europeans to encounter cockatiels were probably the members of Captain James Cook's crew during his three voyages to Australia. One of Cook's officers described a bird that he called a "crested para-keet"—probably a cockatiel—to

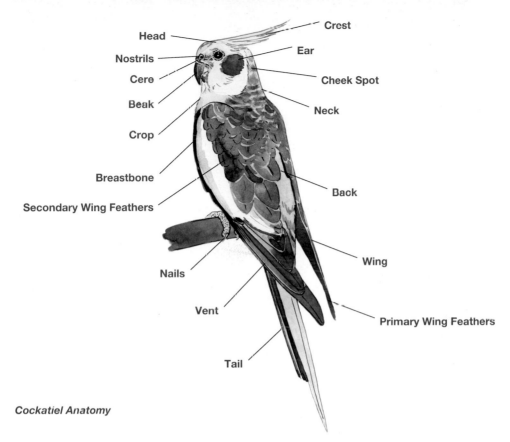

Head

Nostrils

Cere

Beak

Crop

Breastbone

Secondary Wing Feathers

Nails

Vent

Tail

Crest

Ear

Cheek Spot

Neck

Back

Wing

Primary Wing Feathers

Cockatiel Anatomy

British ornithologist John Latham in 1781. Cockatiels were first classified by Scottish writer and naturalist Robert Kerr in 1792. Kerr was working on classifying different kinds of animals according to Carolus Linnaeus's system of taxonomy. He called these small birds *Psittacus hollandicus*—*psittacus* is Latin for "parrot" and *hollandicus* is from one of the early names that the Europeans gave to Australia, New Holland. A later scientist, Johann Georg Wagler, reclassified the birds into their own separate genus, *Nymphicus hollandicus,* in 1832. *Nymphicus*

is taken from the nymphs in Greek mythology, beautiful woodland creatures who usually lived near rivers and springs.

Cockatiels at a Glance
Scientific Name: *Nymphicus hollandicus*
Native Habitat: Australia
Longevity: up to 20 years or more
Length: 12–12½ inches (30–32 cm)
Weight: 2.8–3.5 ounces (80–100 g)
Talking Ability: Limited

Nymphicus hollandicus is the scientific nomenclature for cockatiels to this day. The word cockatiel comes from the Dutch word kakatielje, which reportedly means "little cockatoo." Cockatiels are commonly referred to by different names in different parts of Australia—"weeros" in Western Australia, "cockatiels" in Victoria, and "quarrions" in New South Wales. "Weero" and "quarrion" are the Australian aboriginal words for the bird.

The first cockatiels were brought to Europe in 1840 as pets by John and Elizabeth Gould, a pair of English naturalists who went to Australia to study and sketch birds for a series of heavily illustrated bird books. Their cockatiels were so beloved that when a portrait of Elizabeth was painted following her death in 1841, she was depicted holding a cockatiel.

While illegal smuggling is a problem for some types of parrots, it's really not an issue with cockatiels. Because they breed so prolifically in captivity, it's not worth the time, effort, cost, and risk of trying to smuggle a cockatiel into or out of a country. So when you purchase your pet, you will not be directly affecting the wild population of cockatiels, and you won't unknowingly buy a wild-caught bird, which would be too instinctually fearful of people to ever make a suitable pet.

Cockatiels today are the second most commonly kept type of pet bird after budgies (which are commonly called "parakeets" in the United States). This is in part due to the fact that both birds are prolific breeders, both in and out of captivity, which keeps their cost down. But just as important is their personality—cheerful, interactive, and sweet. If you're looking for a pet that is small, easy to care for, and truly enjoys being with you, you couldn't do any better than a cockatiel.

Chapter Two

Is a Cockatiel Right for You?

As with any pet, it's risky to generalize. A secondhand bird may become an adoring, much-beloved pet, whereas a hand-fed baby may be a disppointment. The best approach is to take the time to get to know an individual bird before you decide to take it home. This chapter will give you an overview of what you can expect with a typical cockatiel in order to help you decide if cockatiels meet your personal requiremonts in a pet.

Pet Potential

Cockatiels' sunny personalities, small size, relatively low cost, and hardy natures have all contributed to their Immence popularity. In fact, a few years ago *Bird Talk* magazine did a survey of its readers, and of all the pet birds out there, the cockatiel was voted "Best Bird of All Time." The poll revealed the same results from both pet bird owners and veteran bird breeders. But cockatiels are not for everyone, and it's far better to be aware of the pros and cons of cockatiel ownership than to make an impulsive purchase that both you and the bird will later regret.

Ask most cockatiel owners what they like about their pets, and they'll tell you that it's the cockatiel personality that appeals to them. Cockatiels are almost invariably cheerful. They enjoy interacting with their owners and they genuinely seem to *like* being with people.

Cockatiels are exotic and provide much of the cachet of bigger parrots without the high-strung natures or destructive beaks. They come in a variety of colors and mutations, but they should never be purchased simply to enhance the décor. Cockatiels are intelligent birds that need stimulation and interaction. Not only would it bo unfair to purchase a oockatiel and then leave it in its cage and ignore it, but doing so may result in both emotional and behavioral problems. A cockatiel is a pet, not a decoration.

Personality

If you are lucky enough to buy a bird that's already tame, you've got a potential instant best friend. Tame

cockatiels love to spend time with people, having their heads scratched, being talked to, and going for shoulder rides. Cockatiels enjoy just sitting with you or perching on your shoulder, preening your hair while you watch television. And nothing will cement the bond between you faster than sharing your snacks with them!

Cockatiels don't have to be hand-fed to be tame. A baby who is handled quite a bit by people but fed by its parents will turn out just as tame as one who is hand-fed. But be careful when purchasing a bird that's not already tame. Trying to tame a flighty cockatiel can be a long and frustrating process, but at the same time, winning the bird's trust is a uniquely satisfying experience. It's up to you to decide whether or not you have

the patience to undertake training an untamed bird. If you're not sure, then it's worth the time and extra expense to find a cockatiel that is already tame.

Size

Part of the reason cockatiels are so common as pets is their size. Roughly the size of a blue jay at about 12½ inches (32 cm) long, they don't necessarily require a large cage. This doesn't mean that they don't need a fair amount of room; the more hours your cockatiel is likely to spend in its cage, the larger that cage should be. At a bare minimum, the cockatiel has to have enough room for short flights without coming into contact with the cage walls or bumping into toys. A suitable cage will take up a couple of square feet of space. For more on cages, see Chapter Four.

Longevity

Cockatiels have a life span comparable to that of a dog or a cat. A typical pet cockatiel that is fed a nutritious diet and receives regular veterinary checkups may live up to 20 years, although there are reports of individual birds living up to the age of 30! As more is learned about optimum nutrition and medical care, it Is reasonable to expect that the life span will continue to increase in the future.

Temperature Requirements

When it comes to temperature, cockatiels have the same requirements that you do. They're most comfortable at temperatures of 65–75°F (18.3 23.8°C). It's not a good idea to keep them any place where the temperature goes below 55 or above 90°F (12.7–32.2°C). If the temperature in a room is uncomfortable for you, it's probably going to be uncomfortable for your bird as well.

Mess and Dust

If you aro the sort of person who is compulsive about being clean and neat, a pet bird is probably not a good choice for you. Birds in general are messy pets, and cockatiels are no exception. They will drop husks, crumbs, and bits of food when they eat, they molt their feathers, and they don't particularly care where or when they poop (although some

people have successfully "potty trained" their birds; see page 73). Cockatiels think it's great fun to push things off a tabletop or to put little triangular bite marks into whatever paper they come across. (Some people actually get their cockatiels to "sign" their Christmas cards along with the rest of the family by letting them bite the bottom of the card.)

But cockatiels are even messier than most other parrots. Like all members of the cockatoo family, they shed a great deal of dander in the form of a fine dust that quickly forms a thick layer on the surround-

problems such as severe allergies or asthma. For people who suffer from these conditions, cockatiels are probably not the best choice as a pet.

The Noise Factor

Cockatiels are very vociferous. The males tend to vocalize more, with long runs of tweets and trills, but the females' voices are heard as well, in short chirps of one to three notes at a time. In fact, in young birds and in mutations where the males and females look identical, it's pretty easy to get an idea of an individual's gender just by listening to its vocalizations.

Some people find cockatiels to be loud, while others don't mind their volume at all. I compare the cockatiel's volume to the voices of the wild birds outside—loud enough to be heard at a short distance, but not overwhelmingly loud. I have, on occasion, had to turn the television up because I couldn't hear it over the cockatiel in the room, but in general, it's not so loud as to be objectionable. If you live at close quarters with your neighbors, they'll probably know from the sound that you've brought home a new bird, but it probably won't be loud enough to bother them.

To some extent, how loud the bird will be may depend on the household it lives in. If the bird is surrounded by noisy children, arguing teenagers, and a blasting radio or television, it may well raise its voice to be heard over the din.

ing floors and furnishings. As a result, frequent dusting and mopping of the room where the bird is kept is necessary. Because of this, cockatiels may not be the ideal pet for the fastidious housekeeper.

Allergies

Cockatiels produce a great deal of dander and dust, and it's not unusual to see a cloud of dust fill the air every time the cockatiel shakes itself off. This is natural for the cockatiel, and while regular misting and bathing may help to reduce the dust, they cannot completely eliminate it.

This dustiness is a particular problem for people with respiratory

Will It Talk?

Cockatiels can talk—but most of them don't. If you want a pet bird that is likely to greet you in your own language, a cockatiel is probably not the bird for you.

Nearly all of those who do speak are males, frequently males who were hand-fed and raised away from other birds so that human speech was all they heard. They generally manage to say a handful of words, but rarely more than that. Females who speak are very rare.

Male cockatiels are very good whistlers, however, and can learn whole songs if they hear them often enough. Many cockatiel owners report that reruns of the old *Andy Griffith Show*, with its whistled theme song, set their birds off into a frenzy of accompanying notes and rifts as they try to whistle along.

Many cockatiels, instead of talking, sort of whistle and chirp their way through words. You'll hear the correct number of syllables and stresses within the phrase so that you know what they're trying to say, but they never quite manage to articulate it. It's suggested that if you want to try to teach your male bird to speak, you should not teach it to whistle first.

Cockatiels and Kids

When asked if cockatiels make good pets for children, my answer is a qualified "yes." In truth, it depends on the individual child, the individual bird, and the parent involved. As a teacher, I've known kids who were very capable and responsible bird owners at seven years old, and I've known teenagers whom I wouldn't trust with one.

We got our first cockatiel when my youngest daughter was five years old. She grew up with them, was always supervised with them when she was younger, and is very

Is a Cockatiel for You?

Pros

1. Cockatiels are relatively small in size and do not take up a lot of space.

2. Tame cockatiels are friendly and outgoing.

3. Cockatiels, when tame, tend to be gentle enough to be handled by a careful child.

4. Male cockatiels can be taught to whistle songs.

5. Cockatiels are relatively inexpensive when compared to other members of the parrot family.

6. A healthy and well-cared-for cockatiel may live for up to 20 years, and possibly even longer.

7. Cockatiels are relatively hardy birds and not prone to getting sick.

8. A cockatiel will stay friendly and affectionate toward its owner even if given a companion bird.

9. A variety of different colors and mutations are available.

Cons

1. Cockatiels need a fairly large cage.

2. Cockatiels need daily out-of-cage time during which they interact with their owners.

3. Although a few cockatiels may learn to talk, you should assume that it probably never will.

4. Cockatiels cannot be left unsupervised with other household pets.

5. The initial cost of cage, equipment, and vet visit can quickly add up.

6. Cockatiels are messy birds that produce large amounts of dander, which becomes airborne when the bird moves, covering the nearby floor and furnishings with a layer of dust that requires frequent cleaning.

7. Cockatiel dander may irritate people with allergies or asthma. They are one of the worst possible pet birds for households where someone has one of these conditions.

8. Cockatiels are one of the easier birds to breed in captivity, and a pet hen may frequently lay and incubate eggs, even if there's no male to mate with.

comfortable handling them. Now that she's a teenager, the cockatiels love her and will sit on her shoulder and preen her hair while she does her homework. Contrast this with another family who asked me if I'd take in their "vicious" cockatiel. I had my reservations, but went to see the bird anyway. As soon as we entered the room, the bird rushed to the floor of the cage, where it crouched and hissed menacingly. One of the children hurried up to the cage ahead of his mother and me, yelled at the bird, and banged on the side of the cage while the mother said nothing. It didn't take a bird expert to figure out why the bird was "vicious." I decided then and there to take the bird with me. Seven years later, I can handle him, but he's still not good with children and never will be.

For a responsible, empathetic child, however, a tame cockatiel can be an excellent pet. A tame cockatiel is gentle, attentive, and will willingly stay on its owner's hand or shoulder while indoors, observing the activities of the household or repeating short tunes that are whistled to it. Children can not only take responsibility for their bird's daily maintenance, but can also exercise their creativity by constructing toys for their bird to play with.

The very same traits that make cockatiels suitable pets for children make them ideal for senior citizens as well. Cockatiels make lively, interactive companions for anyone who lives in a place where dogs and cats are not allowed.

Cockatiels and Other Pets

Cockatiels can live with other pets, but doing so requires a great deal of vigilance on the owner's part. Cockatiels should never be out of their cage unsupervised in the presence of a dog, cat, or ferret. All of these animals instinctually view the cockatiel as prey, and even the best-behaved dog or the most sedentary old cat can experience a momentary lapse—and that's all it takes to be the end of your cockatiel.

Cat bites pose a particular threat to cockatiels. Beyond the bite itself, cat saliva contains a kind of bacteria called *pasteurella*, which is fatal to birds. Even if the bird survives the initial attack, it is still vital that the bird be seen by a veterinarian as soon as possible to determine whether or not there was a puncture wound and to administer a lifesaving dose of antibiotic, if necessary.

As for cockatiels and other birds, if you decide to have them in the same household, the problem is most likely to come from the other bird. Cockatiels are fairly gentle and usually will not act aggressively if properly introduced. A second cockatiel is not likely to be a problem, although there are exceptions. (The abused cockatiel that I rescued, for one, attacks any other bird that nears his cage and has to be housed alone for the safety of the second bird.) Smaller, non-aggressive species can also successfully share cage space

with a cockatiel; for example, we have a Bourke's parakeet who has shared a cage with a cockatiel hen for several years. Aggressive birds, however, should not be allowed near a cockatiel. Even smaller birds such as budgies or lovebirds will go after a cockatiel—in spite of the fact that the cockatiel is double or even triple their size—because their species are naturally aggressive.

Some people worry that the addition of a second bird, particularly another cockatiel, might negatively impact the first bird's relationship with the owner, or that the bird will be so attracted to its new companion that it will stop interacting with people altogether. Actually, this isn't likely. Over the years my cockatiel flock has changed several times as birds have come into my house and then left to find their permanent homes. Not once have I had a friendly bird become any less interactive with me because of the addition of a new member of the flock. The exception to this is if a nest or eggs are involved. Both cockatiels may become very defensive of the nest, but once the eggs hatch, both parents will go back to the way they were before they became parents. If anything, adding a second (or third or fourth) cockatiel makes the new bird more inclined to bond with me because it sees how much the first bird enjoys the time it spends with me.

This holds true whether you begin with one cockatiel and then add another at a later date, or if you decide to get two at the same time. One bird or two, cockatiels are charming pets.

Chapter Three

Are You Right for a Cockatiel?

On one hand, cockatiels are fairly easy to care for. They don't take up a lot of space, you don't have to walk them when it's cold outside, and their droppings are relatively small and easy to clean up. On the other hand, they are intelligent birds who need daily attention and interaction from their owners in order to be happy. A neglected bird may develop undesirable habits, such as screaming in order to attract attention or pulling out its own feathers. So before you decide to bring a cockatiel into your home, you need to examine your lifestyle in view of the bird's needs in order to make sure that you're a good match for a cockatiel.

Cost

After finches and budgies (which are commonly referred to in the United States as "parakeets"), cockatiels tend to be the least expensive birds in the pet store. They usually cost even less if they are acquired from a breeder, or you may find a "bargain bird" at an animal shelter, through an ad in the newspaper or on the Internet, or because you know someone who no longer wants his or her bird and is seeking to re-home it for free.

So a pet cockatiel is a real bargain, right? Well, maybe yes and maybe no.

To get an idea of what acquiring a cockatiel will initially cost you, see the checklist of necessary equipment on page 28.

Beyond the initial cost of the cockatiel and the necessary equipment to keep one, you should also consider the ongoing expenses of both packaged food and fresh fruits and vegetables (although most of the fruits and vegetables that you eat are perfectly fine for the bird, if you care to share your leftovers with it). You should also include the cost of cuttlebones or mineral blocks, replacing toys as they become chewed down and worn out, and incidental veterinary bills for the next 15 to 20 years. Cockatiels may be one of the more inexpensive pet birds, but one cannot really call them "cheap."

Space

You might think that a small bird won't take up much space, but considering that your cockatiel will probably spend most of its time in its cage, it needs a fairly large space to live in. To keep the bird happy and healthy, the cage should have enough space for the bird to spread both wings out simultaneously without touching the cage on either side. Ideal arrangements have more than one perch so that the bird can fly from one to the other in order to get some exercise. Add to this the space you'll need for toys, dishes, and a cuttlebone, and it soon becomes clear that a cage designed for a parakeet, finch, or canary is not going to suit your cockatiel.

A suitable cockatiel cage for a single cockatiel should have a perimeter no smaller than 20 × 20 inches (50 × 50 cm), but larger is better. If you want to get a cage with a "skirt" that extends beyond the perimeter to contain the mess, or if you decide to leave a couple of inches of free space on all sides of the cage as a "dust and debris zone," your little bird may take up more space than you first anticipated.

Time

Some birds, such as finches and canaries, serve well as "decorative accessories"—they can be perfectly happy living in your house, adding to a pleasant atmosphere with their beauty and song and requiring a minimum of interaction with you beyond being fed, watered, and cleaned on a daily basis. Cockatiels are not like that. Cockatiels are intelligent and social birds that thrive on interpersonal interaction. They like to watch you, they like it when you talk to them, and they love it when you take them out of the cage to scratch their heads or hold a special treat for them to eat. Cockatiels, particularly single cockatiels, simply aren't happy to be shut up in a cage and ignored.

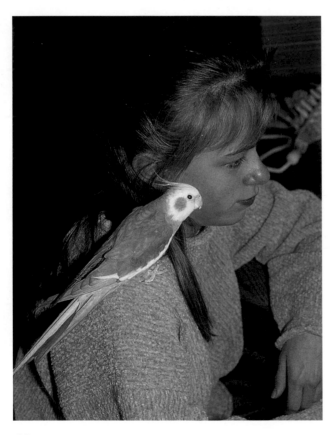

A tame cockatiel needs to spend approximately an hour a day outside its cage. It can be either interactive time, when you are actively holding it, talking to it, and scratching its head and neck, or passive time, when you let the bird sit on your shoulder, preen your hair, and watch what you're doing.

If you are a person who is seldom at home, or who spends days or even weeks at a time traveling for work, you may not be the best person to own a cockatiel. If you are at home but busy with children, entertaining, or working from home, you may also want to reevaluate whether or not you can give a pet cockatiel the time and attention that it needs.

Other Considerations

Other, more minor factors may influence whether or not you are a good match for a pet cockatiel. Because they can't use their feet like hands, as some bigger types of parrots do, they like to explore things with their mouths. As a general rule, these explorations are limited to a gentle nibbling, but if you are uncomfortable with the thought of being nibbled by a curious cockatiel, you might want to either meet and handle one before you commit, or rule cockatiels out as a prospective pet. People with freckles are particularly susceptible to being nibbled and tasted, sometimes a little harder than

they might like, as the bird tries to remove the offending freckle, which it considers a speck of dirt that needs to be cleaned up.

This well-meaning nibbling also extends to jewelry. Cockatiels love to nibble on bright, shiny jewelry, and may well tug on your earrings, pinch your skin while trying to get to your ring, or even break a thin chain on a necklace. If you like to wear jewelry, consider whether or not you would be willing to take it off before you pick up your cockatiel.

Nibbling extends to hair as well. Cockatiels aren't able to reach the feathers on their heads and necks, so they preen each other, gently running the feathers through their beaks and tonguing them to help get them clean and to break open new feather sheaths. Because your bird likes you and wants to help you stay pretty, it may very well preen your hair given half a chance. If you're very particular about your hair and would not be

comfortable having it rearranged by a miniature feathered hairdresser, you might want to reconsider your choice of bird.

Re-Homing Your Bird

There may be a time when, for whatever reason, you have to find your cockatiel a new home. If it's honestly in the bird's best interests, then do everything you can to find it the best new home possible. It's better to give the bird up than to keep it in a situation that's less than ideal. It should go without saying that you're responsible for the bird's health and well-being until it actually finds its new home. Simply turning an unwanted cockatiel loose doesn't mean you're setting it "free" — it means that you're casting it out into a place full of predators where it has

no idea how to survive. If you don't want or can't keep the bird, you have several options for finding it a new home.

Many breeders and pet stores will take the cockatiel back if you find that you're not able to keep it, no matter how much time has elapsed and no matter what the reason for your giving it up. You won't get a refund or exchange, of course, but you'll know that your bird is going to a safe place.

If returning the bird to the source isn't possible, you still have several options. You can try to find a new owner by word of mouth, letting your acquaintances know that you've got a cockatiel up for adoption. Frequently coworkers or relatives know people who would love to bring the bird into their household, and this gives you the security of having someone who will vouch for the reliability of the cockatiel's new caregiver.

If you can't find someone who's willing to take the bird this way, try advertising in the newspaper or on the Internet. Write the ad clearly, describing the bird, it's gender, and whether or not it's tame. If you're giving up the bird for personal reasons, such as allergies or because the original owner has passed away, say so in the ad so that potential owners will know that you're not giving it up because of any undesirable behavior on the bird's part.

To help ensure that your bird goes to a good home, you might want to list a small adoption fee in the ad. This helps to make sure that the cockatiel will go to someone who truly wants the bird rather than someone who's responding to an ad for a free bird on a whim. You don't actually have to charge the fee if you find the right prospective owner, but knowing that he or she would be willing to pay will help reassure you that the new owner would also be willing to spend money on fresh foods and veterinary care, should the need for it arise.

If you decide to sell the bird through an ad, it's a good idea to tell any prospective owners that, because several people responded to the ad, you would like to meet them and have them meet the bird in order to find the best possible match. This way, if a person arrives who is obviously not going to be a responsible bird owner, you don't have to come up with an excuse as to why you won't let them have the bird.

Ask any prospective owners about previous cockatiel experience, how much they know about cockatiels, whether or not they have a cage and its accessories already set up to receive the bird, the name of their veterinarian, whether there are any other pets in the house (particularly ones that might prey on crested little birds), and why they want a cockatiel. Introduce them to the bird and see if they're comfortable handling it and whether or not the bird seems to like them. Don't be disappointed if the bird tries to get off of them to fly to you—it just means that the bird is more familiar and comfortable with you. It can learn to love the new owner just as much in time.

If you don't want to advertise for a new home for your cockatiel, there are many animal shelters and bird rescue groups that will take the bird. Although you sometimes hear about organizations that take in unwanted birds and then turn around and sell them at a profit, this usually isn't an issue with cockatiels, which are so plentiful and inexpensive that unscrupulous groups don't want to deal with them. To be certain that you're surrendering your bird to a legitimate adoption organization, look for one that has 501(c) nonprofit status. These groups have to meet certain government standards to be considered tax exempt. Although a great number of private rescue organizations do not have 501(c) status, those that are so designated are more likely to be respectable groups operating for the best interest of the birds they take in, rather than for profit.

As long as we're talking about responsibility and the need to re-home birds, it's a smart idea to make arrangements in advance for your cockatiel and any other pets in the event of your death. Decide who of your family and friends would make a good bird owner and talk to that person about the possibility of taking your cockatiel in after you die. God willing, you won't need him or her, but you can finalize the arrangement by officially leaving the bird to the person you select in your will.

Chapter Four
Getting Ready

Sometimes it's impossible to prepare in advance for a pet cockatiel. You might rescue a lost bird, inherit one from a relative who passes away unexpectedly, or receive one as a gift from a well-meaning friend. When this happens, you have to scramble to get everything you need. Even though you do the best you can in those situations, it's much easier and less stressful for both you and the bird if you have everything ready before bringing your new friend home.

Cage

A lot of bird breeders, when asked how big a cage a cockatiel needs, respond, "Get the biggest cage you can afford." This is basically a variation of "the bigger the better." The larger the cage you can get for your bird, the more room it will have for exercise, and the happier and healthier it will be. That said, there are a few other factors you should take into consideration before selecting a cage. As a general rule, the cage that most people start out with is the cage the bird has for the rest of its life, so this is not a good place to cut corners.

You want a cage that's safe for your bird. The first factor to look at is bar spacing. If the bars on the sides of the cage are too far apart, you run the risk of the bird getting its body caught between the bars, which can result in serious injury. A cockatiel's cage should have bars that are no more than a half inch apart from each other. It doesn't really make a huge difference if the bars are vertical or horizontal, as long as they aren't too far apart.

Some bird owners feel that round cages can be disorienting, and that when a bird is feeling anxious or stressed, it likes to have a corner to retreat to, something that's lacking in a round cage. You should also avoid cages with sides that bulge out farther than the perimeter of the base; they look attractive, but if the bird is perched on the outermost part of the cage and poops or molts, the mess will end up on your floor or table instead of inside the cage.

The size of the cage is very important. The more time you antici-

pate your bird will stay in its cage, the bigger the cage should be.

For a single cockatiel, a good minimum size is 20 inches × 20 inches (50 cm × 50 cm). For each additional cockatiel, it's a good idea to increase the size of the cage by 30 to 50 percent. A cage that is wider than it is tall is good, because birds fly vertically, not horizontally, but these can be difficult to find.

Look for a cage with a large door that swings open so that you can reach in with your whole arm. The reason for this is that if you ever need to take an injured or frightened bird out of the cage, it is much easier if you have full access to the cage,

rather than having to twist your arm through a small access door.

For ease of maintenance, it's also better to have a cage with a small door over each dish. It's less intrusive and makes it easier for you to get the dishes in and out of the cage without spilling. The closer to the cage floor the food dishes are, the less likely spilled food and excess husks are to fall out of the cage and onto your floor.

Some of the newer cages don't come with bars at all, but are made of a thick plastic all the way around, which allows a nearly unobstructed view of your beautiful bird and keeps most of the shells, husks, feathers, and dander *inside* the cage. I'm not particularly fond of these because they don't offer convenient places to hang things like toys, cuttlebones, and extra dishes. I also worry that they tend to be a bit more humid than the traditional cage in spite of ventilation holes, and the clear sides tend to show fingerprint smudges— and worse—both inside and outside the cage, requiring more cleaning than the traditional barred cage.

Secondhand Cages

Be wary of secondhand cages, which can pose a variety of hidden dangers. Older cages, or cages that are imported from foreign countries, may contain toxic metals; bars may contain lead or zinc, the solder may contain lead, or parts of the cage could be painted with lead-based paint. Exposure to these metals may lead to irreversible brain damage, just as it does in humans.

Another risk of secondhand cages is possible exposure to germs and disease. If the last bird who occupied the cage died of a disease, the cage may still harbor the germs that caused that disease. Some diseases, such as psittacosis, are transmitted in the dust that comes from dried bird droppings, and these bacteria can remain active for months.

If someone offers you a second-hand cage, ask what happened to the last bird that lived in it. Even if the bird wasn't lost to disease, it's best to treat any secondhand cage with either a disinfectant recommended by your veterinarian or a

mix of one part bleach to nine parts water. You can soak the cage in the bleach and water solution for fifteen minutes, or wipe the cage down with the solution, and then rinse it from the top to the bottom with clean water.

Cage Placement and Lighting

Birds need light. The number of hours of light they receive every day helps to regulate their sleeping and breeding cycles. Exposure to light is necessary for the bird's physical and emotional well-being and helps to foster a happy, healthy bird. Parrots need exposure to vitamin D_3 for the same reason humans need exposure to vitamin D—it's crucial for the absorption of calcium in the body. Like people, parrots can absorb this crucial vitamin through exposure to natural sunlight, particularly ultraviolet light, but because most pet cockatiels are kept indoors, they frequently suffer from a vitamin D_3 deficiency, which results in bone deficiencies. Exposing your bird to sunlight through a glass window is not a sufficient substitute for natural sunlight; the windowpanes filter out the crucial ultraviolet light, making it ineffective as a source of vitamin D_3.

If you live in a place where the weather is warm, you can remedy the situation by situating your cockatiel's cage so that it sits partially in the light that comes through a screened-in window. (You always want to leave a part of the cage in the shade so that the bird can get

Windows filter the natural lighting that cockatiels need to process calcium.

out of the direct sunlight if it starts to feel too warm.) A closed-in screen porch also provides a good opportunity for the bird to "catch some rays," as long as you make sure that the door to the outside is locked to prevent people from opening it unknowingly and letting the bird escape.

If you live in a cooler climate, special steps need to be taken to ensure that your bird gets sufficient exposure to ultraviolet light. Specially designed full-spectrum electric lights emit the ultraviolet light that your cockatiel needs when it's too cold out to expose it to natural sunlight. These lights are different from the ordinary incandescent, fluorescent, or halogen types of lightbulbs, which don't emit ultraviolet light.

These full-spectrum bulbs are available either individually or as part of a lamp with reflectors designed to steer beneficial rays toward the bird. They can be found either in a pet shop, online, or through a pet supply catalogue, and the package will clearly indicate that they are "full-spectrum."

Ultraviolet lights should be set up in such a way that both the light and its cord are out of reach of the cockatiel. The package directions will tell you how to set up the light in order to best meet your bird's needs.

Cage Cover

A cage cover is an optional accessory. Some people feel that their cockatiels sleep better if they're

Do-It-Yourself Play Stands

We had a commercial play stand at my house for a while, but we found it was big and awkward to move from place to place, and difficult to stash when we wanted it out of the way. So we came up with two separate play stands of our own, made up of common household items.

A very quick and inexpensive play stand can be made of any type of basket that has a handle. Line the inside of the basket with paper towels for easy cleanup and tie one or two hanging toys from the handle for the bird to play with. For a treat, you can also attach a spray of millet to the handle and let the bird have at it. The millet makes a royal mess, but most of the husks fall into the basket below, which makes it much easier to clean up.

For multiple cockatiels, we use a collapsible wooden clothes drying rack which can be found at many department and hardware stores. We simply set the rack up over spread-out newspapers to protect the floor, and tie toys to the different rungs, attaching dishes that come with metal brackets to the side of the rack for food and water. Not only is this a fairly inexpensive way to make your own play stand, but when company is coming over, you simply take off the dishes and collapse the entire rack, toys still attached, and stow it in the closet until the next time you need it.

in a darkened cage in a quiet room. If your bird wakes up earlier than you'd like and tends to vocalize, a covered cage can also fool it into thinking that it's still dark out and staying quiet. In addition, if you have a female that's a chronic egg-layer, covering the cage at night may trick the bird into thinking that the nights are longer, and therefore that it's not the proper season to nest.

A cover can be as simple as a sheet or towel tossed over the cage. Covers can also sometimes be found in pet supply stores, or, if you are a crafty sort, you can buy your own material and sew your own cage cover, using either a material with a bird print or one that matches your room's décor.

If you want to try beginning your bird ownership without a cage cover, you may find that you get along just fine. I don't cover my own cockatiels' cages and it's never been a problem.

Play Stands

Some cages come with a play stand attached to the top. A play stand is a series of perches, frequently with dishes, toys, ladders, or swings attached, for your bird to play on when it's out and standing on top of the cage. Play stands can be useful if you want to give your bird a break from its cage but are unable to physically hold it. Cockatiels can be trained to stay on the play stand by simply returning them to the cage every time they venture off of it.

One caveat about play stands: Be sure to get one that is short enough that the bird is lower than your eye level while standing on the highest perch. This is because some cockatiels that look down on their owners get the idea that they, the birds, are in charge, and behavior problems may result. The theory is that, in the wild, the most important bird in the flock gets to perch on the highest (and thus safest) branch in the tree, and so they associate height with power. Either way, it's easier to enjoy the bird if it is at eye level or lower.

Play stands also come separately from cages and consist of an easy-to-clean platform with the same perches and toys that a cage-top play stand might have. These are useful if you want to have your bird with you in different rooms but the cage is too large to be easily moved from room to room.

Perches

Most cages come with a couple of wooden perches. While these are functional, they are usually not the ideal arrangement for your bird.

Cockatiels literally spend almost all of their lives standing on their feet, and since most perches that come with cages are all the same diameter, the bird's foot is in essentially the same position as long as the bird is sitting on a perch. This is not good for the muscles in the bird's feet. As a rough analogy, imagine a woman who was forced to wear three-inch-high heels twenty-four hours a day, seven days a week, and was never able to take them off. Eventually some of her muscles would be stretched out while others would atrophy as a result of not being used. The same sort of thing happens to the bird.

So it's important to have perches of at least two different diameters in the cage. Perches come in a variety of sizes and materials, and there are pros and cons to each. It may be difficult to figure out which kind your cockatiel prefers—birds tend to want to sit on the highest available perch no matter what it's made out of.

Wooden perches: Many cages come with plain wooden dowels for perches. These are attractive and convenient because they come with the cage. The disadvantage is that most of these dowels are made of a soft wood, such as pine, which the birds enjoy chewing on. This chewing is actually a good thing—it helps to keep the bird's beak from overgrowing—but it also means that you may eventually have to replace the perch, or the bird may chew right through it!

Some manufacturers make wooden perches that are undulated like the spindles of a railing and whose diameter varies along the length of the perch. These are good because the bird's foot will automatically change its grip to accommodate the varying diameters of the perch. But again, this type of perch is often made of wood, so it's susceptible to chewing and may need to be replaced eventually.

Natural branches cut from the outdoors work well, if you have trees that you know are free from pesticides. Before placing a branch from outdoors in your cockatiel's cage, you should first wash it off with hot, soapy water (be sure to rinse all of the soap off afterwards!), then put it in the oven at 150 degrees for 45 minutes to an hour, to make sure that you kill off any insects or bacteria living on the branch. I have apple tree branches in one of my cockatiel cages on the theory that they might be sweeter and more fun for the birds to chew. Some people like to drill a hole on the cut edge of the branch in order to install a bolt that can be used, along with a washer and a wing nut, to fasten the branch to the side of the cage, but my own preference is to simply wedge the branch securely in the cage bars.

Manzanita branch perches: Some pet stores and supply catalogues offer manzanita branch perches. Manzanita is a shrub or small tree that is native to western North America. It's extremely hard and quite resistant to small, chewing beaks. It's usually sold with hardware attached, and its twisting, angled branches make it visually

Perches that mimic branches are a good choice and promote healthy feet.

very interesting. Manzanita branches come in a variety of sizes, from small twig-like pieces that are appropriate for a cockatiel to large, thick branches that are suitable for the biggest macaws. The piece you choose should be appropriate for the space you have in your cage. Manzanita perches tend to be pricey, but they're also very durable and long lasting.

Sandpaper-covered, cement, and plastic perches: Some compa-

nut to attach them to the side of the cage, and the far end is usually slightly tapered so that the heaviest section is closest to the cage bars. While they are less irritating than the sandpaper, I haven't found them to be effective in keeping toenails worn down. I have to trim my cockatiels' toenails even when they have a cement perch.

Plastic perches are available, but I'm not a big fan of them. They are fairly easy to clean, but are frequently too smooth for the bird to get a comfortable grip on. This is particularly true for very young birds, who are pretty clumsy anyway.

Rope perches: Another type of perch is a rope of braided cloth around a flexible wire core. On either end, a plastic screw affixes to the side of the cage. These perches are usually colorful, and they are flexible enough to be bent into different shapes. You can bend them into corners, loops, zigzags, or other configurations as opposed to a straight line that goes from one side of the cage to the other. Changing their shape will keep things interesting for both you and your bird. Many people feel that the fabric on this type of perch is the most comfortable for the bird's feet. The one downside to these flexible rope perches is that the threads in the cloth braids (which are usually cotton) do wear down under the stress of the bird's pointy little toenails, and sometimes threads eventually break loose. These threads can eventually become entangled in the bird's feet,

nies sell sandpaper-covered or cement perches that are supposed to keep a bird's toenails worn down. Sandpaper-covered perches are not advisable because they tend to irritate the bird's feet after a while. (Think about it—would you like to constantly stand barefoot on sandpaper?) Cement or concrete perches come in different diameters, and in a variety of sizes and colors. They come with a bolt, washer, and wing

resulting in injury. As the perch ages, it's important to check it for loose threads, which should be cut off, and to replace the perch when it starts to become too worn.

Most perches can be placed in different positions in the cage. Two things should be taken into consideration when you decide where you want to put them. The first is that you need to leave enough room between the perch and the cage for the bird. Don't put it so close to the top, for example, that the bird has to crouch to sit on it, or so close to the side that there's no room for the bird's tail between the perch and the side. The second is that you want to make sure that the perches are not over the food or water dishes or toys. Not only is having bird droppings in the food and water unhealthy, but it is much easier to keep toys and dishes clean to start with than to have to scrape the droppings off later!

Cuttlebones and Mineral Blocks

Birds need calcium for the same reason as people—in order to develop and maintain strong and healthy bones. But unlike mammals, birds do not make milk, nor can they ingest the lactose that it contains. So captive cockatiels need to get their calcium from a combination of two different sources: either from a cuttlebone or a mineral block, and from the foods they eat.

A cuttlebone, as the name implies, is the internal skeleton of the cuttlefish, a cousin of the octopus and squid. Because it's more porous than the bones of other creatures, it's soft enough for birds like budgies and cockatiels to chew off small bits with their beaks. The cuttlebone is made largely of calcium carbonate, and it provides an excellent and easily digestible source of calcium for birds.

A specially formulated mixture of minerals (including calcium) and vitamins that is processed into a solid block, mineral blocks can be chewed on and ingested by birds help meet their nutritional needs. They come in a variety of colors, flavors, and shapes.

My birds tend to prefer cuttlebones to mineral blocks, but I'm not sure if it's because they prefer the taste or the texture. Theoretically, the mineral block may be healthier for them, but it's not useful if they won't use it, so I keep both in their cages at all times, just to make sure they get the necessary calcium. I'm still trying to find the brand and flavor of mineral block that they like best. Since I know that cockatiels tend to prefer vegetables to fruits, I get vegetable-flavored blocks rather than fruit-flavored ones.

Whether you use a cuttlebone or a mineral block or both, it's very important that they be carefully situated inside the cage. They should be affixed to the bars of the cage rather than placed on the floor, where they can become covered with droppings. Fasten them to the inside of the cage near a perch so that your cockatiel can reach them easily. Mineral blocks usually come with fasteners that make it easy to attach them to the cage bars. Cuttlebones come either in packages, which will contain a holder that you can use to attach them to the cage, or loose, in which case you can buy a separate holder that you can reuse if you want to save money or be environmentally correct. Because cuttlebones are quite porous, it's also possible to drill holes in them and just tie them to the side of the cage.

Both cuttlebones and mineral blocks come in a variety of sizes. I tend to buy the smaller ones, which last for quite a while, because they block less of the cage wall, giving my cockatiel and me a better view of each other.

Other Supplies

Dishes and Water Bottles

As a general rule, the dishes that come with cages are perfectly fine. They are safe, durable, and serve their purpose. The glitch comes when you need three dishes—one for dry food, one for moist food and/or fresh foods, and one for water. Most cages come with only two dishes.

One way around this is to use a water bottle. Water bottles are not only convenient, but they also can't be contaminated by droppings, odd bits of food, and cockatiel dander.

Checklist of Supplies

Necessary
✔ Cage
✔ Assorted perches
✔ Cuttlebone or mineral block
✔ Toys
✔ Extra dishes or water bottle
✔ Food
✔ Full-spectrum lighting (if no exposure to natural light)
✔ Find an avian veterinarian

Optional
✔ Play stand
✔ Carrier
✔ Cage cover
✔ Postal or diet scale

There are three disadvantages to using water bottles. They can be difficult to clean, and you will need to buy a brush designed for scrubbing the inside of baby bottles to do so effectively. Many cockatiels have never seen a water bottle before, and so you'll need to keep a traditional dish of water available at all times until you see your cockatiel actually drinking from the bottle. It may take a while, but cockatiels are curious and like to explore things with their mouths, so they will eventually figure it out—it's frequently just a question of how long it takes you to realize that your bird knows how to drink out of it. The third disadvantage is that cockatiels like to bathe occasionally, and if you do opt to give your bird a water bottle, you'll need to offer it a shallow bowl of water every few days in case it wants a bath (pie plates work really well as makeshift birdbaths).

Most pet stores and catalogues sell dishes that can be used if your birdcage only comes with two dishes. Because moist foods or fresh fruits and vegetables will start to spoil, these foods should generally only be accessible to the bird for an hour or two. The best arrangement, if you don't use a water bottle and your cage only comes with two dishes, is to use the third, free-standing dish for the fresh or moist foods, setting it in the cage so that it's not directly under one of the perches and removing it after an hour or two. You can also set the third dish full of fresh food on the play stand or cage roof to be enjoyed during your bird's out-of-cage time.

The dishes themselves can be plastic, stainless steel, or ceramic, although if you use a ceramic dish, make sure that it's not coated with a lead-based glaze. As a rule, if it's safe for you to eat off of, it's safe for your cockatiel. At my house, we frequently use custard cups or ramekins for the third dish—they're just right for cockatiel-sized portions.

Another option for dishes is a "ring and crock" arrangement, where a metal ring screws to the side of the cage and a small dish sits inside the ring. While these are convenient because you can situate them almost anywhere in the cage, there have been reports of cockatiels trying to fit through the ring while the owner has the dish out to wash or refill it. The birds or their wings can get caught in the empty ring, resulting in broken bones or other injuries. So if you do opt to use this kind of dish, when you need to remove it, unscrew the bracket of the ring and remove the entire assembly, both ring and dish, instead of leaving the empty ring in the cage. Or, simply take your cockatiel with you when you remove the dish from the ring.

Whichever type of dishes you use, remember not to place them directly under perches, to avoid the droppings falling into the food and water.

Bedding

To make your bird's cage easier to clean, you'll want to use some sort of bedding at the bottom of the cage. A variety of different materials are available, but for me, the one that works best is plain old newspaper. I take the paper, open it up, and trace out the size and shape of the tray that goes in the bottom of the cage. I cut it to fit exactly, then place all of the layers of the shape I've cut into the cage. Every morning, I remove the top layer of newspaper, revealing the next clean page underneath. It's a fast and easy way to keep the cage clean.

One word of caution, though. While most of the commercially sold substances for the bottom of the cage are just fine, you should never use corncob bedding, walnut shells, or kitty litter. Although all of these materials are absorbent, they are not digestible and may clog the bird's digestive system, resulting in its death. Since it's not unusual for a cockatiel to explore things by tasting them, keep these particular beddings away from your bird and its cage.

Toys

People with no bird experience might think that toys for birds are a waste of time and money. Not true! Cockatiels love their toys. They manipulate them, beat them up, snuggle with them, scold them, love them, and swing from them. It is entirely possible that you will never see your bird playing with toys—

it may stop when it hears you approaching because it would rather play with you. So just because you don't see your bird playing with its toys, don't assume that it doesn't use or enjoy them. You never know what goes on when you're not in the room!

Of the wide variety of toys available, it's hard to predict exactly which ones will appeal to a cockatiel. Toys made of plastic, wood, leather, metal, cloth, palm frond, and cast-off household items all make delightful diversions for the caged cockatiel, and different cockatiels will have different preferences. Trial and error is the best way to discover exactly what kind of toy your cockatiel prefers.

The ideal cockatiel toy will be small enough for the bird to get its beak around. Most pet stores and catalogues identify toys according to the size of bird they're best suited for—budgie, cockatiel, conure, macaw, and so on. If they don't, look for toys that say they are intended for "small" birds.

Cockatiels are like small children when it comes to toys—they'll have their favorites and ones that they don't like, and after a certain amount of time passes, they may get bored with the toys they have. For this reason, it's a good idea to buy several toys and rotate them in the cockatiel's cage every week or so. This way, the bird enjoys the excitement of a "new" toy at regular intervals and the individual toys last longer.

Most cockatiels seem to enjoy toys that hang from the ceiling of the

cage. They bat at them, swing on them, and chew them. Avoid toys that hang from an S-shaped clip; there have been cases where cockatiels have gotten the end of the "S" hooked under their beaks and hung helplessly until their owners rescued them. Instead, use clips that close to attach the toys to the cage. Bells can be a pleasant addition to toys, but be careful not to choose "jingle bells"—round bells with a slit in the side—because your cockatiel's tongue or toes could get caught in the slit, causing them to bleed.

Making your own toys can be great fun as well. You can either buy the parts you need separately— wooden blocks or beads with holes drilled into them, plastic beads that are ready to string, and leather thongs or cotton string to bind the pieces together—or you can assemble your toys with bits and pieces that you find in your own home. Shoelaces, old keys, odd game pieces, dried-out pens, and the like all make intriguing parts for constructing cockatiel toys.

Making homemade toys is a great way of including children in caring for the family cockatiel. Not only does it foster creativity in children, but they get a real sense of pride and accomplishment when they see their cockatiel playing with the toys that they made.

Food

Although diet will be discussed in detail in Chapter Nine, it's generally a good idea to find out what kind of food your new cockatiel eats before you take it home and secure a supply of it to have on hand when your bird arrives. This will make the bird's transition that much less stressful; if you are planning to make a significant change to its customary diet — whether it be a switch to or away from pellets, or a change in brand, flavor, or mixture — it is entirely possible that the cockatiel will refuse to eat the unfamiliar new food.

Familiar foods are comforting and can make a new situation just a little less stressful. Find out what your cockatiel is used to eating and buy a small supply of an identical food to help ease the bird's transition to its new home.

Carrier

A carrier isn't an absolute necessity, but it is a good idea. If you buy your cockatiel at a pet store, they will probably send it home in a flimsy cardboard carrier that's basically a box with punched-out air holes. For a short trip home, this is adequate, although being stuffed in a dark box may be scarier for the bird than riding in a carrier with a view. Cardboard carriers also are not durable, and if your cockatiel is in one for any length of time, it may well start chewing at the punched-out air holes. Thin cardboard is no match for a determined cockatiel beak, and given long enough, your bird may very well chew its way out.

If the bird soils the box on the trip home, you should discard the box afterward, even though this will leave you without a carrier to use on future trips. Even if you don't intend to travel with your bird, it's still a good idea to invest in a suitable carrier not only for the trip home, but for trips to the veterinarian, to the bird sitter's, or in case you ever have to evacuate your home.

Carriers or crates intended for dogs and cats are generally not suitable for a cockatiel. The bars on most dog and cat crates are too far apart, and a cockatiel could get its head or wings caught between them. If you do opt for a carrier with bars, the same rule of thumb that applies to cages still applies: the bars need to be no more than a half inch apart.

Because cockatiels' beaks are not as powerful as those of other birds, carriers for a cockatiel can be made out of a wide variety of materials; plastic, wood, nylon, screen, and cloth are all suitable. Adjust the size of the carrier according to how long you expect the bird to be inside. If you anticipate making frequent long trips with your bird, you'll want to opt for a bigger carrier than someone who only anticipates making annual trips around the corner to the veterinarian. The carrier should be big enough for the bird to stand comfortably and to turn around.

Shipping a bird: The carrier you choose is largely a matter of personal preference. One exception to this rule is if you anticipate having to ship your bird by plane. Fortunately, cockatiels are so readily available that you should be able to find your ideal bird without having it shipped from a breeder thousands of miles away, but if you do have to ship a

bird by plane, airlines have very specific regulations about the kind of carrier you must use. The sides have to be solid and able to withstand the weight of another parcel falling on top of the carrier, and most airlines require that there be some kind of perch for the bird fastened to the inside of the crate. Size regulations should be obtained in advance from the airline.

If you do have reason to ship a bird, look for a carrier with a lock to keep the bird from being lost or stolen en route. In shipping other birds, I've used wooden crates that screwed shut and could not be opened without a screwdriver and carriers that were fastened with a padlock. It's also a good idea to leave a supply of fruit, such as grapes and orange sections, in the crate so that the bird has a supply of nourishment and moisture in the event of a missed connection or a cancelled flight. If you are relocating across country and are planning to travel by plane yourself, taking the bird as your carry-on baggage is the best option when possible. Doing so greatly reduces the stress and risks to the bird because you keep it with you at all times. However, different airlines may have different regulations. Most will require you to have a health certificate signed by a veterinarian before they'll let your bird on one of their planes, or they may charge you a fee for taking the bird into the cabin with you. Make sure you contact your airline well in advance of traveling with your bird to be sure that you comply with all regulations before arriving at the airport.

Scale

Also optional, but recommended, is a scale that can be used to weigh very small objects. This is helpful because sick birds tend to hide all signs of illness until they are literally too sick to hide them anymore. They do this instinctively to keep from making their weakened state obvious to predators. Unfortunately, this same instinct means that they're going to try to hide their illnesses from *you*, and so by the time you realize that there's a problem, the bird's health may already have deteriorated past the point where medicine can help.

The one symptom of illness that a bird can't hide is weight loss, and so it is recommended that cockatiel owners weigh their birds every few days to monitor any changes. Your bird's weight will normally fluctuate by a few grams every day, so a gain or loss of a gram or two isn't a cause for immediate concern, but a steady decrease in weight over time or a sharp drop in just a few days should be taken as a sign that the bird needs to be seen by a veterinarian.

Because cockatiels are so small, their weight should be measured in grams—your typical bathroom scale is not sensitive enough to effectively monitor the weight of a cockatiel. Although there are scales with perches attached that are specifically designed for weighing birds, scales designed for dieters or for weighing postage are generally less expensive and easier to find. I use a postal scale that I bought at a local office supply store. It gives weight in either ounces or grams, and the reading is displayed in large, easy-to-read numbers on an LCD screen. I simply have the bird stand on the platform, push the button, and write the number down.

The average range for a cockatiel's weight is between 80 and 100 grams ($2\frac{1}{2}$–$3\frac{1}{3}$ ounces). Like people, some cockatiels will be a little bigger and others a little smaller, and some may be underweight or overweight. Beyond comparing your bird to this weight range, you can also get an idea of whether or not your cockatiel is within a healthy weight range by examining its chest. A bird that's at a good weight will not have an indentation in the center of the chest where the keel bone is, giving it the appearance of having "cleavage"; nor should the breast be so thin that the keel bone is prominent and can be easily felt sticking out from the chest muscles.

Veterinary Care

I strongly suggest that any new pet be taken to the veterinarian for a general checkup within 48 hours of its arrival. Not only is this frequently a condition of any guarantees—if you realize later that your bird has a health issue, you'll be out of luck—but if the bird needs to be returned, you want to do it before you get too emotionally attached.

Any veterinarian can call himself an "avian veterinarian" and treat birds, but only a handful are specially trained to treat birds. These specially trained experts are called "certified avian veterinarians" and are certified by the American Board of Veterinary Practitioners as having taken special courses in avian medicine in veterinary school. The key is to look for the word "certified"—that shows that you have a real expert.

Because there are relatively few certified avian veterinarians, they may take a little extra effort to find and be located farther away than you'd anticipated, but it's generally well worth whatever extra time and effort it takes in terms of the quality of care your bird receives. If you can't find a certified veterinarian in your area, the Association of Avian Veterinarians maintains a list of veterinarians, both certified and not, who accept birds as patients at *www.aav.org*.

You can use either the Internet or references from other bird owners to find a good veterinarian in your area. I recommend that you find your veterinarian in advance and make an appointment for your bird as soon as possible. I try to make the first appointment coincide with the time I intend to bring the bird home. Not only does this mean one less stressful trip for the cockatiel, but it also ensures that any potential health problems are found sooner rather than later, providing an extra layer of protection for both you and any other birds you may have at home.

The first veterinary visit is important even if your bird is perfectly healthy. The results of any lab work that your veterinarian orders will help to establish what is normal for your bird and give the veterinarian a basis for comparison for all future visits.

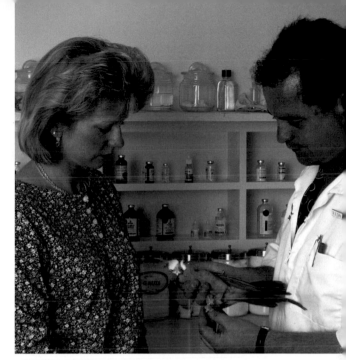

Finding an avian veterinarian can be difficult but is one of the best things you can do for your bird.

Things You Don't Need

Some pet stores will sell you a "Cockatiel Starter Pack" that allegedly contains everything you need for your cockatiel. It seems like a great deal—the price of the combo is less than the price of the individual items—but these packages are frequently stuffed full of things that you don't really need. Here are a few things that you can do without.

Gravel and grit: There are many types of birds that need to eat sand or grit in order to grind down their food, but parrots are not among them. Not only are gravel and grit

your bird does not have mites when you acquire it, and you do not let it go outside or come into contact with an infested bird, in all likelihood it will never become infested by them. Therefore, you probably don't need a device to keep your bird mite-free. Also, some mite protectors contain pesticides, and it's best not to expose your bird to them if you don't have to.

Sandpaper-covered perches: These are supposed to help keep your bird's toenails worn down, but their effectiveness can be offset by the diameter of the perch. They also irritate the bottoms of the feet more than they help with the toenails.

Vitamins: There may be times when a vitamin or mineral supplement is necessary, but if your bird eats a healthy diet supplemented by nutritious foods intended for humans, your bird may be able to make do without them. A veterinarian can give you personalized advice as to whether or not vitamins will benefit your bird, but there are two considerations to keep in mind. Powdered vitamins will trickle down if sprinkled on dry food, and vitamins added to drinking water can foster the breeding of potentially harmful bacteria in the bird's water supply. It's better to feed a healthy diet to start with than to add supplements to a poor one.

unnecessary for cockatiels, but they can be downright dangerous. Grit can become impacted in the bird's digestive system, killing the bird if it's not relieved.

Mite protectors: Mite protectors are small metal disks that are hung from the side of the cage to ward off mites, small, blood-sucking insects that can cause your bird to itch to distraction. They even may cause the bird to pull out its feathers, and sometimes even rip open its skin, in an effort to relieve the itching. But if

Chapter Five

Choosing Your Cockatiel

There are many different ways that people come to be cockatiel owners. Some people do weeks of research trying to come up with just the right bird for their lifestyle; others meet a bird unexpectedly and it's love at first sight; and still others find themselves owners of a pet cockatiel after adopting a lost bird, or taking one in for someone who can no longer care for it. No matter how you acquire your cockatiel, the more you understand and interact with your new bird, the better and happier your relationship will be.

What to Look For

No matter what kind of bird you decide to look for or where you buy your bird, you want what every pet owner wants—a bird that is tame, interactive, and healthy. If this is your first bird, you may have no idea what to look for when picking out your new pet. A few simple things can help you tell a good choice from a poor one.

First, observe the environment. Is it clean and neat? Are the food dishes full, the water clean, and the bottom of the cage relatively free of accumulated droppings? Are the birds kept in a location that allows them to observe people on a regular basis? Are there toys and mineral blocks or cuttlebones available for the birds? You want a bird that looks like it's had the best of care.

Observe the birds. They should be alert, bright-eyed, and active. They may flutter when you first enter the room but should calm down fairly quickly. They should be interested when you approach the cage and seem to listen to you when you talk to them. Sudden moves may startle them, but they should recollect themselves nicely.

The seller should be able to handle the birds and should allow you to handle them as well. A well-socialized bird can be coaxed into stepping onto an extended index finger when it hears the words "Step up" (or something similar) and the side of the finger nudges the chest just in front of the bird's legs. Birds that do not let themselves be handled can be tamed down with time and effort, but it's easier to start off with a bird that's already used to being handled.

Don't be disappointed or put off if you try to handle a bird that has caught your eye and it keeps watching the seller, trying to get to him or her while you're holding it. Cockatiels are a lot like small children and frequently want to go to the person they already know rather than staying with a new person. If you bring the bird home with you, eventually you will become that familiar person. As long as it comfortably lets the seller handle it, the bird demonstrates the potential for being an excellent pet.

Where to Find Your Bird

If you make a conscious decision that you want to acquire a cockatiel, there are many different options available: pet stores, breeders, animal shelters, and ads from newspapers and the Internet looking to re-home unwanted birds. You may find the perfect bird through any of these sources, but there are pros and cons to each, and you need to consider these factors before you decide where to go.

Breeders

Breeders can be found by looking on the Internet, in the classified section of newspapers, or in parrot magazines. There are several advantages to buying from a breeder. Because they breed the birds, they are familiar with the bird's bloodlines, sometimes going back for several generations, and they know the bird's medical history from birth. They also know the personalities of the birds they have for sale and can help steer you toward the one with the kind of disposition you're looking for, whether you'd like the friendliest, most outgoing baby in the clutch, or the sweet little quiet one who is happiest sitting perched on your shoulder.

Birds bought directly from the breeder are much more likely to have been hand-fed, played with, and socialized, thus making them tame, affectionate pets from the very start. Birds bought directly from the breeder also tend to be less expensive than birds from a pet store—there's no overhead to pay and they cut out the middle man.

Never purchase a cockatiel that is unweaned. The unopened pinfeathers on the head of this bird say that it's too young to be sold yet.

Pet Stores

Pet stores offer the advantage of being local and easy to find, and they usually offer a variety of different mutations. Most pet stores are respectable businesses that take excellent care of the animals they sell; the employees take time to know and socialize their birds and therefore can help steer you toward your ideal pet. Look for a pet store that's clean and where the birds seem alert, active, and happy. The staff should be knowledgeable about cockatiels and able to answer all of your questions. A reputable store will offer some kind of guarantee about the quality of it's birds and may offer a printed handout with information on cockatiels that you can take with you, whether you buy a bird or not. One of my own little tricks is to ask if the birds are ever given fresh fruits or vegetables. A "no" doesn't necessarily mean that the birds or the store are inferior, but a "yes" suggests that the store goes that extra step to make sure its birds are both happy and healthy.

Secondhand Birds

It makes sense that, if cockatiels are one of the two most popular kinds of pet birds, they would also be one of the top two species that are most frequently offered for sale or put up for adoption either when their original owners no longer want them or are no longer able to care for them. Getting a secondhand cockatiel is a bit of a risky proposition. Something about the bird made the owner give it up; you have to make sure that that "something" is something you can live with.

Secondhand pets are a real wild card. Sometimes you get a wonderful pet; sometimes you get one with significant behavioral or health issues. Two of my cockatiels were secondhand birds. Charlie, the abused bird I mentioned in Chapter Two, is still nervous, flighty, and likely to bite any hand that reaches into his cage. Hannah, a pearled cockatiel hen that someone found on the street and turned into the

Starting with a bird that was handled as a baby may allow you to bond with it faster.

Massachusetts Society for the Prevention of Cruelty to Animals' Western New England shelter, was missing a few feathers in places, but she was so friendly and affectionate that the staff all adored her and would take her out of her cage and into the break room to spend time with her. I frequently take Hannah into schools when I give talks about birds because she's so calm and friendly toward everybody. Two secondhand cockatiels, two very different results.

The first question you should ask when looking at a secondhand cockatiel is, "Why is this bird being given up?" The answer will give you some indication as to whether or not this particular bird is what you are looking for. If the answer is that it bites, it's too loud, too messy, or some other negative, proceed carefully. If you're looking for a companion that you can live with for the next few decades, you want to choose carefully.

There's no substitute for actually meeting and handling a bird before you commit to bringing it home, and this is especially true with second-hand birds. What one person calls excessive loudness might only rank as background noise to you. And there may be mitigating circumstances with a bird who bites—the person it's biting may remind it of an unpleasant experience in its past, or it may be afraid of the blood-red nail polish the person wears.

Disabled Birds

You should avoid adopting a sick cockatiel at all costs, but disabled birds are another matter altogether. Because there are a wide variety of disabilities, the pet potential of a disabled cockatiel varies as well. A bird that is missing a leg, a wing, or toes can still be a delightful pet, depending on the individual bird.

We own one cockatiel with splay legs. His parents' owner didn't think that the eggs his hen laid on the cage floor would hatch, even though there was a male bird present and they took turns sitting on the eggs. When the baby hatched on the hard cage floor, his legs were forced to go in opposite directions when he sat, and because the owner was afraid to move the chick, he ended up splay-legged—instead of having two legs that stick out straight under him, he can only stand with one leg straight and the other sticking out to the side. Once weaned, he came to live with us. We don't usually handle him because his balance is a bit shaky, but he shares his cage with another male and likes to take treats from our hands, whistles to us, and happily lets us scratch his head.

In other words, a disabled cockatiel can still make a delightful pet and should not be ruled out simply because of special needs. It's hard to generalize about accommodations that need to be made for a bird with a disability because there's such a wide variety of disabilities. Use common sense. Consider how the bird is disabled and what about its environment might produce difficulties, then try to solve the problem. A visually disabled bird, for example, shouldn't have the fixtures in its cage rearranged, and you should talk to it when you enter the room so that it isn't startled when you reach the cage. A bird with one leg will do better in a cage with horizontal bars than with vertical ones, which are harder to climb. A bird with impaired balance will be less likely to get hurt if the perches are arranged lower, rather than higher, in the cage.

If you don't think you're up to the task of caring for a special needs bird, then by all means don't adopt one, but don't rule a disabled bird out until you've considered the pros and cons of owning it.

Making Your Selection

Sometimes you do a lot of research and figure out exactly what it is you want in a bird, and sometimes you simply stumble across the perfect bird who makes it clear that you're the one *it* wants. Be flexible. Do your research and head out to meet a bird, but if you find a bird that appeals to you even though it may not be the gender or mutation you were looking for—or if you meet a bird that seems to really like you and tries to get to you even when other people are holding it—be open minded. You're looking for the perfect bird, but the perfect bird may not be the one you were expecting.

Gender

I'm frequently asked which make better pets, males or females. My answer is that neither one is "better" than the other, but there are differences. Normal males are more colorful than normal females, although when you're looking at hybrids, the difference in their plumage may be less marked.

No matter what they look like, males are much more vocal than females. The difference is so distinctive that breeders rarely have their birds DNA sexed—they can often tell which gender an individual is even before the adult plumage comes in, based on the sounds the bird makes. Males like to sing songs that go on for several bars, either repeating songs they've learned from you or from other birds or improvising their own jaunty tunes. Because they are more vocal, males are more likely to learn to talk, although cockatiels are not known for their talking ability. Cockatiel speech will never be mistaken for human speech because their voices are high pitched and whistle-y.

Females also vocalize, but they generally just chirp a couple of notes and then they're done. I've heard of female cockatiels who've learned how to talk, but I've never met one. They're just as sweet and friendly as the males, but they're quieter about it. We don't keep male cockatiels in the same room as the family television because they tend to try to be louder than whatever show we're watching to get our attention, but

we've occasionally kept females there.

Male birds also have an advantage in the fact that they don't lay eggs, whereas a female may, even if there's no male present. The laying of eggs in and of itself is not a problem, but it does tax the hen's body because some of her calcium and

other nutrients go toward the formation of eggs, weakening the hen somewhat. In rare cases, hens may also become egg bound, which is a serious medical emergency and needs immediate veterinary attention. Egg laying is not a certainty with lone female cockatiels, but it is ono moro pioco that you might want to consider before deciding whether to buy a male or female bird

Age

Some cockatiel owners prefer to acquire young birds over adults. There are several reasons for this. A young bird is less likely to have picked up bad habits, such as screaming and biting, and is more likely to adapt smoothly to your household. But older birds can make excellent pets, too, and in many mutations, you can tell the sex of an older bird simply by looking.

Although age isn't as important as the personality of the individual bird, if you do decide to adopt a young bird, it's never a good idea to buy one that's less than eight to ten weeks old, the approximate age that the baby bird finishes weaning. The idea that the baby will bond more closely to you if you hand-feed it isn't true; cockatiels are very social

able to feed the bird at regular intervals both day and night.

If you make any mistakes in hand-feeding, it's the baby cockatiel who will suffer. Never buy a baby that is not weaned and avoid any breeder who offers to sell you one— he or she clearly does not have the bird's best interests in mind.

Hand-fed vs. Parent-Fed

A hand-fed baby makes a good pet, but that doesn't mean a parent-fed baby is necessarily an inferior or less social pet. I will occasionally hand-feed a baby if it looks like the parents have more than they can manage (and because baby cockatiels hatch every other day and grow very fast, the youngest baby generally isn't big enough to compete with its siblings for food and often dies). But for the most part, I let the parents do all of the feeding, taking the babies out daily to be handled and given a chance to get used to people. Not only is this safer for the babies, but it spares me from having to get up every two hours at night to hand-feed them.

Babies that are handled from the beginning grow up perfectly comfortable being with people, no matter who feeds them. The tricky part comes when dealing with a bird that has never been handled. These birds can usually be tamed to the point where they can be handled and become affectionate pets, but it takes a lot more time and effort. The key is to meet and try to handle any bird before you buy it. If the bird is

birds, and your bird will not be more attached to you as an adult if you feed it as a baby. Hand-feeding a baby bird if you've never done it before is a very risky proposition. Make the formula too hot and you may burn the baby's throat and crop; make it too cool and the baby will refuse to eat it; accidentally get formula into the lungs rather than to the crop and the bird will die of drowning or pneumonia. You also may not be able to judge when the baby is full and you need to stop feeding it, or you may not be avail-

Left to right: a normal gray male, a cinnamon female, a lutino, and a normal gray female.

calm and lets you handle it, then it doesn't really matter how it was fed as a chick.

Mutations

As mentioned before, wild cockatiels are primarily gray. Over the years, however, breeders have manipulated pairs to emphasize or de-emphasize different characteristics in the plumage. There are now several different color mutations and combinations of mutations available for sale. There's no difference in terms of pet potential—all of these mutations are the same size and are equally suitable as companion birds. It's just the colors that differ.

Because the different mutations can be mixed together into countless new combinations, and different organizations have different standards or different names for what is essentially the same mutation, the passage below will discuss the most commonly recognized mutations. Others exist, but they are either extremely uncommon or are not universally recognized as separate mutations.

Normal Gray

Normal gray cockatiels look the same as the original wild cockatiels did when European explorers first arrived on the continent of Australia. The body is all gray, with white on the outer edges of the wings. There

The patch of yellow on the back of this normal gray hen indicates that she is a split and carries the genes for a different mutation.

are round orange "cheek" spots over the ears in both males and females. (The birds' ear location is pretty much the same as it is on you; on the side of the head, just a little lower than the eyes. If you part the feathers on the cheek spots, you can see the little hole that is the entrance to the ear.) For about the first nine to ten months, both males and females look alike—their heads are primarily gray tinged with yellow—but as they mature, the males' faces become bright yellow, while

the females' stay essentially gray. Males' tails also turn solid gray, whereas the females keep the barred pattern on the underside of the tail that all young normal gray cockatiels have.

Lutino

A lutino is a bird that, because it received a recessive gene from each parent, lacks some of the pigments found in a normal gray. As a result, the bird is pale yellow with orange cheek spots and red eyes. Young lutinos and females have a light barring pattern on the underside of their tails, while male lutinos have solid white there, but otherwise it's difficult to tell the bird's sex visually. A lutino is similar to an albino, and many birds that appear to be albino are in fact white-faced lutinos, a combination of two different mutations. Because the gene for -ino mutations (lutino and albino) is both recessive and sex-linked, birds who have these mutations are more likely to be females, although males are possible.

Although lutinos are very attractive birds, there is what could be termed a genetic fault that goes with this mutation. Lutinos frequently have a bald patch on the top of their head just behind the crest. Sometimes this is so small as to be barely noticeable; other times a large patch is involved, and the bird looks like it was plucked on the top of its head or like there is something wrong with it. This bald patch is normal and permanent. It has no effect on the bird's health or personality. A lutino with a bald patch on the top of its head is just as healthy and affectionate as other cockatiels; it's just a little less attractive.

There is one other quirk worth mentioning about cockatiel mutations, like the lutino, that have red eyes. The red eyes result from a lack of pigment in the eyeball, which causes the birds to be somewhat

more sensitive to light than the dark-eyed varieties. These cockatiels will probably be more comfortable in a room with softer lighting.

Pearl

A pearled pattern of feathers on a cockatiel might more accurately be called "scalloped." In this mutation, some of the feathers on the body are edged with white or yellow, giving them a scalloped appearance. This mutation is the opposite of most others in that the females and

Male pearl chicks lose most of their distinctive markings when they mature.

The distinctive white marks on this bird are called "pearling."

the young birds are the ones who demonstrate the more attractive appearance. Almost all male pearls lose their pearl markings after their first molt, so it's the young and the females who are the most attractive.

Pied

A pied cockatiel is one with patches of color. The patches may be gray, white, yellow, or pearled. There's no particular formation to these patches, which may be large or small; you can't gauge a pied

bird's gender according to its plumage, since a young bird or a female may have the same bright yellow face as a male. If you pick a young pied bird with pretty pearl patches, keep in mind that pearl markings fade in male birds during the first molt, and those pearl patches might end up plain gray once the bird matures.

Cockatiel breeders recognize different classifications of pied markings. A bird that is mostly yellow with gray patches is termed "heavy pied," while a bird that is mostly gray with yellow patches is called "light pied." A cockatiel that is pied to the point where it is completely yellow is called "clear pied"; these birds differ from lutinos because their eyes are black rather than red.

Cinnamon

Cinnamon cockatiels are light brown in color rather than gray. Female cinnamons' faces are a bit more yellow than a normal gray hen's would be. In adult males, the underside of the tail is solid rather than barred. Because the cinnamon mutation is a sex-linked trait, cinnamon cockatiels are more likely to be female than male.

Fallow

A fallow cockatiel resembles the cinnamon mutation with the exception of having red eyes. This mutation is recessive rather than sex-linked, and so while both of the bird's parents must have the recessive gene, males and females will be equally affected.

Silver

Silver cockatiels are a lighter gray color than a normal gray bird and have red eyes. This mutation is caused by a recessive gene.

Yellowface

A yellowface cockatiel lacks the orange cheek spot, giving it a solid yellow face. It's a sex-linked mutation, meaning that you see it only in male birds, although females can carry and pass on the mutation.

Whiteface

As its name implies, a whiteface cockatiel lacks the yellow face as well as the orange cheek spot and has white in their place. Whiteface males will develop a fully white face after their first molt, while females merely develop a faint wash of white on their faces. Because this mutation is caused by a recessive gene, it has to be inherited from both parents. Whiteface chicks have a white down when they are hatched instead of the usual yellow.

Splits

A split is a bird that is a combination of two or more mutations. Some split mutations may be present genetically but may not be apparent in the bird's physical appearance. For example, two parents that look like normal grays may actually be splits, and some of their offspring may turn out to look markedly different from their parents.

Although this bird may look albino, it is actually a white-faced lutino.

Signs of an Unhealthy Bird

It's not enough to find a bird that meets your list of desirable qualities or that seems to really like you; just as important as finding a bird that you want is finding a bird that is healthy. Birds can be very tricky when it comes to visually gauging their health. In the wild, predators are most likely to single out a bird that looks the least able to flee successfully. Therefore, wild cockatiels do everything they can to hide all signs of illness. In general, by the time the bird can no longer hide an illness and the owner realizes that the bird is sick, it may be too late to save the bird.

This natural inclination to hide signs of illness poses a special problem for the first-time cockatiel owner, who may not know what's normal and what's a sign of illness. Here are a few key things to watch.

Behavior

A healthy cockatiel will be lively, alert, and curious about the world around it. It will sit erect on it's perch, chirp happily, and probably raise its crest in curiosity when you approach. Avoid birds that sit dully, especially if they are on the floor of the cage rather than the perch. (Young birds that have not yet learned to fly may sit on the floor of the cage, but in this case it's a sign that the bird is still too young to be sold, a question of development rather than a sign of illness.) Inactivity is a bad sign.

Feathers

An adult cockatiel should be fully feathered, and the feathers should lie smoothly against its body. Birds sometimes regulate their temperature by fluffing out their feathers; a

The fact that the head feathers are plucked indicates that another bird is responsible for the feather loss. Note the pin feathers coming in.

A pair of cockatiels will preen each other. In the absence of a second bird, it's up to the owner to preen the head and neck.

bird whose feathers are all puffed out may be running a fever, and this should be considered a possible sign of illness.

Missing feathers may be caused by the bird pulling its own feathers out or being overly preened by a well-meaning cage mate. Birds that pull their own feathers may do so because of an illness, infestation by mites, or behavioral issues—all of which are good reasons not to purchase that particular bird. Birds that have their feathers plucked by a cage mate may be perfectly healthy, but you need to be sure that it's the second bird that's responsible for the missing feathers. If the bird's body is plucked, but not its head, the culprit is probably the bird itself. If the head is plucked, it's probably a case where the cage mate caused the damage, since cockatiels can't

reach to preen their own heads.

Frayed tails are not necessarily a sign of trouble, especially if you're looking at a young cockatiel that's housed with other youngsters. Like any human toddler, young cockatiels are innately curious and like to explore things by putting them in their mouths. It's not uncommon for one curious youngster to try to taste the tail of another. Tails can also be frayed when they are inadvertently rubbed between the bars of the cage.

Lutinos and albinos may have a bald spot just behind the crest, but otherwise missing feathers should be taken as a warning sign that something may be amiss.

Droppings

Normal cockatiel droppings look like long, coiled green tubes surrounded by a white covering. They are solid, well-formed, and not watery, and should not contain any undigested seed. The vent area should be clean and dry and not have any waste sticking to it. Cockatiels don't really urinate and defecate the way that mammals do. All body waste is produced simultaneously and consists of three parts: The tubular part of the droppings is the feces, the white part that makes a sort of lacy covering on the feces is the urates, and the very small amount of clear, odorless liquid is the urine.

The bird's droppings can be affected by whatever the bird has eaten. Sometimes the color of the pellets or foods like beets or cranberries will change the appearance of the droppings. The seller should be able to tell you what the bird has eaten recently.

Hens who are about to lay eggs or who already have eggs will "hold it" for a very long time because they don't want to defecate in or near their nest, but at the same time, they don't want to leave the nest any more than necessary. In consequence, these birds will go a very long time between trips to relieve themselves, and the resulting pile of feces is astonishingly large, possibly more than two tablespoons worth of droppings. Because they've held it for so long, the droppings will be wet and messy. While laying eggs is normal for an older hen, if a bird you're looking to buy is about to lay eggs, it's probably not the best choice because they can be quite tenacious in defending their eggs.

Sneezing

As is the case with humans, sneezing can be caused by exposure to dust and other allergens, or it may be a symptom of respiratory illness. If you see a bird you're considering as a pet sneeze, carefully observe the bird, looking for swelling, discharge, or redness around the nares and eyes. If you see any of these, the bird is likely ill and should be avoided.

Environment

You can frequently predict a bird's health by carefully observing its surroundings. Does it come from a clean, smoke-free environment where it is housed in a large, spacious, well-kept cage? Do the members of the household seem to be well informed and intent on the bird's well-being? The surroundings that a bird is kept in can provide a clue as to whether the bird has been well cared for—or not.

Chapter Six

Bringing Your Cockatiel Home

It's best to prepare as much as you can before you bring your new cockatiel home. Set up the cage, make an appointment for a "new bird checkup" with the veterinarian, and stock up on the kind of food your bird is used to. If you have other birds, you'll want to quarantine the new bird as best you can. Personally, I like to give new birds a 24-hour adjustment period before I take them out of the cage and try to handle them. Going to a new home is a major change in their lives—new people, new surroundings, new everything. Giving them 24 hours to observe and adjust will make for an easier transition and a less traumatic homecoming.

Quarantine

If you own other birds, start by setting up a quarantine room for the new bird to live in for the first month you have it. Because birds will hide signs of illness until they are at death's door, you can't assume that a bird is healthy just because it doesn't look sick. Even if you took it

to the veterinarian on the way home from the seller, the veterinarian will probably have taken samples for lab work, and the results of these tests won't be available right away.

A quarantine room should be located as far away from your resident bird as possible. Because most rooms in a house share heating and ventilation systems, complete isolation is difficult, but do the best you can. Be sure to service the resident bird's cage before you take care of the new bird's. By feeding, cleaning, and watering your old bird before you take care of the new one, you avoid carrying any germs or viruses from your new bird to the old one. Be sure to wash your hands after any contact with the new bird.

Cage Location

The location of your bird's cage and play stand can play a big role in the bird's socialization. You want to place them in a location that is both safe and allows the bird to see and be seen by all members of the family. Kitchens, while they tend to be social hubs, are actually one of the worst possible locations in terms of safety, particularly because of the risk of toxic fumes being given off by overheated nonstick pans. Likewise, locations with a straight shot to an outside door are risky even if your bird has clipped wings, in part because of the increased risk of the bird flying out the door (wing clips are not permanent, and if they are not monitored you may be surprised by your bird taking flight) and in part because of the exposure to drafts and sudden drops in temperature when the door opens.

Find a place where the temperature is comfortable, the surroundings are safe, and where the household members spend a fair amount of time so that the bird gets to observe and interact with the family as they go about their business. Living rooms and family rooms frequently make good locations, although if you find that the bird likes to compete vocally with your television, you may want to rethink the placement of the cage. Many birds enjoy being in a location where they can see out a window, allowing them to watch the world outside. However, take care that this doesn't leave the bird exposed to constant sunlight with no available shade in the summer and that it's not too cool or drafty by the window in the winter.

Making Introductions

Cockatiels make an excellent first bird—they're hardy, friendly, and not high-strung like some other parrots tend to be. But what if you already have a bird? Is a cockatiel a good choice for a companion for your current pet?

Well, it depends on what kind of bird you currently have. If it's another cockatiel, there'll probably be no problem. Cockatiels tend to be social and enjoy a companion of their own species. It doesn't really matter if you have two birds of the same gender; they'll still probably get along. Adding a third cockatiel may be problematic, however, as sometimes a bonded pair will resent the intrusion of a "third wheel." Mixed-gender couples also get along well—sometimes a little too well, as cockatiels are very uninhibited when it comes to breeding. Many pairs won't reproduce unless you give them a nest box or some other darkened enclosure to nest in, but every now and then you'll get a pair that will lay eggs on the cage floor and incubate them. This may happen even if you have a single hen, although hers won't hatch. The only way to ensure that you're going to be egg-free is to keep only male birds.

As mentioned in Chapter Two, the success of adding a non-cockatiel as a second bird depends on a number of factors, including the gender, species, and temperament of the individual bird. Because of this, it's recommended that you thoroughly research any potential companion birds for your cockatiel, and that you make sure that each bird has its own cage with several inches between them so that the beak of one bird can't reach through the bars to bite the foot of the other as it clings to the bars of its own cage.

Even if you have two birds that initially seem to get along well, you should give each of them its own separate living space. My daughter bought a cockatiel on the same day that I bought a pionus parrot. The breeder actually recommended this particular pionus because she seemed very interested in the cockatiels. They got along well for about six months, and then one day the pionus started chasing the cockatiel with a gaping beak. We separated

them with no more harm to the cockatiel than a bad fright, but we've never let the two of them out at the same time since.

If you are adding a cockatiel as a second (or third or fourth…) bird in the household, there are a few things you can do to make the transition and introductions easier. While the new bird is in quarantine, always make sure that you take care of your long-time resident birds first. There are two reasons for this. The first is

that your resident bird expects to be your first priority while your new bird doesn't. If, one morning, you suddenly go in to see the new bird when the resident bird is used to being greeted first thing, you increase the risk that your current pet will be jealous of the newcomer, which can make it more difficult for them to get along. The second reason is one of hygiene. If you take care of your resident bird first and the newcomer second, you lessen the chance that you'll inadvertently carry germs or viruses that the quarantined new-

comer might be harboring to your resident bird.

When the quarantine is up and the new bird has been cleared by the veterinarian, you can begin to introduce your pets to each other. First, move the cage with the quarantined bird in it into the same room as your current bird. Place the cages so that they can see and call to each other. Give them a few days to get used to each other, and when you go in to take care of them, continue to tend to the resident bird first. Not only will this keep your resident bird from feeling like its place in your heart is being usurped, but seeing the two of you interacting will also help convince the new bird that quality time with you is a pleasant experience. Over the course of several days, move the cages closer and closer to each other until they are finally right next to each other. If they seem to be getting along okay, and you don't observe any aggressive behavior such as hissing and lunging, try opening the two cages simultaneously, so that the birds can come out and interact. It may be a good idea to have a small towel handy in case you need to break up any fights—tossing a towel over an angry bird before you pick it up can save you from being bitten.

If the two birds get along, you may be able to move them both into the same cage at this point, keeping the second cage on hand in case you need to separate them for any reason in the future. Once you see them preening each other, you can be confident that they've formed a companionable friendship.

Handling Your Cockatiel

The first thing you need to know about a cockatiel is how to pick it up. Never try to pick up a cockatiel by putting your hand around its back and lifting it. This will terrify your bird and probably earn you a bite in return. Being grabbed around the back scares the bird on an instinctive level; when a predator goes to capture a wild cockatiel, it usually does it by clamping down with its teeth or talons on either side of the bird's body from above, placing its mouth over the bird's back. For this reason, cockatiels and other birds panic when grabbed this way.

The best way to pick up your bird is by extending your index finger as if you were pointing at something. For added stability, you might want to extend the middle finger as well. Place the side of your index finger against the bird's chest, just in front of the legs, and gently nudge the chest with an upward motion, saying "Up" or "Step up" or whatever other word you want to use as the verbal cue to get the bird to step onto your finger. If it's been handled before, the bird should recognize what you're asking and will step delicately onto your hand.

You can move while carrying the bird, but try to keep your hand steady and not to make any sudden movements. Some birds will try to clamber onto your shoulder—whether or not you allow this is up to you. There's an old joke that the reason so many pirates wear eye patches is because they let their parrots sit on their shoulders. Leaving your bird on your shoulder does put your face within biting distance, although a cockatiel's beak cannot inflict nearly as much damage as that of a bigger bird. Keeping your bird off your shoulder will also help to keep your clothing clean and free from bird droppings.

If you don't want your bird on your shoulder, simply have it step back onto your hand every time it moves up there. If it persists, return it to the cage. Eventually it should figure out what its boundaries are. The same goes for a bird that wants to perch on your head; if you remove it promptly, it should eventually stop trying to land there.

Personally, I do let my cockatiels sit on my shoulder. It frees my hands and lets them spend time with me while I move about the house, picking up after my kids, folding laundry, and even while I work on this book!

With regard to birds pooping on your clothing, it's largely a matter of personal tolerance. Some people put a small linen towel over their shoulder before letting the cockatiel sit there; others have a specially designated "bird shirt" that they put on before picking up their cockatiel (one lady I know has a special "bird hat" as well). Because I live in a multi-bird household, putting on my work shirt is always the very last thing I do before I leave the house; it's the best way I have to make sure that I don't go to work with any "extra decorations" on the back of my shirt.

Interacting with Your Bird

Cockatiels are not as demanding as other pets. You don't have to walk them, brush them, license them, scoop out litter boxes, or carry their poop through the neighborhood in a plastic bag. These are all plusses. But if you've never had a bird before, you may find yourself standing in front of the cage, or even holding the bird perched on your hand, and asking "Now what?"

It's not a good idea to try to pet a bird the way you would a dog or a cat. Not only does a hand placed around its back remind your cockatiel of predators, but for some birds, being stroked on the back gets them sexually excited, which will lead to a frustrated, unhappy cockatiel. Luckily, there are many other ways to interact with your bird that can be mutually enjoyable. Preening, sharing snacks, and teaching your bird tricks are all good options.

Preening

When a person grows a new hair, the hair springs from the skin fully formed. When a bird sprouts a new feather, the feather pokes through the skin wrapped in a thin, waxy covering called a sheath. This sheath is fairly supple when it helps the feather break through the skin, but it hardens as the feather grows, becoming brittle enough so that the cockatiel can break it up by chewing it, freeing the soft, fluffy part of the feather. For the most part, this is a good arrangement, except for one thing—the cockatiel can't reach the feathers on its head and the back of its neck.

In the wild, cockatiels depend on other cockatiels to help them open the sheath by gently chewing on it. Your pet cockatiel depends on you to perform this task for it, and may even signal that it needs help by facing you and lowering its head to the point that its forehead is almost touching the floor. This posture is an invitation to preen your little feathered friend. If no one has preened the bird in a while, you can actually see the pointy little sheaths sticking out of the bird's face and head — when your bird looks like a cross between a cockatiel and a porcupine, it's past time to preen the bird.

Preening is actually pretty easy. Start by simply scratching the bird's head with your fingernail. Since the sheath can be quite itchy, your bird will probably enjoy the sensation and will probably close its eyes in bliss and tilt its head in order to give you better access.

Some of the sheaths will be thin and easy to break open, while others, especially near the back of the neck, will be thicker and may not break open with a simple scratch. These need to be cracked open by squeezing or piercing them with your fingernail and thumbnail. There are nerves in the sheath when it first breaks through, and if you try to break open one of these thicker sheaths too close to the skin and before it's hardened, the bird may emit a sharp squawk and pull away, possibly even giving you a bit of a peck. You might think that you've hurt the bird, but this is actually more of a warning than a threat, and within seconds the bird will probably lower its head again, asking you to continue.

Don't be surprised if your bird attempts to preen you in return. This is a normal, pleasurable activity to the cockatiel and one that it naturally wants to share with you. If the bird nibbles on your hair, eyebrows, or beard, this is preening. It's not painful and it makes the bird happy. Mutual preening sessions are an excellent way to bond with your new pet.

You may notice, when you watch your bird preening itself, that it will rub its beak just above where the tail meets the body and then proceed to wipe its beak on the feathers all over the rest of its body. The bird is rubbing the uropygial gland, or "preen gland," which produces an oil that cockatiels use to keep their feathers clean, shiny, and water resistant.

Head Rubbing

In addition to the necessary preening, many cockatiels enjoy having their heads scratched and their faces rubbed simply because they like the feeling. The back of the neck, just over the cheek spots, and under the chin are all favorite places to rub and scratch if you want to make your cockatiel feel good.

Shoulder Rides

Being curious birds, cockatiels like to observe everything you say and do. Many people take their cockatiels around the house with them as they do their daily chores, with the birds perched happily on their shoulders. You'll be surprised just how tenacious cockatiels are at clinging to your shirt as you bend to make a bed or reach to pick up a dustpan full of dirt.

If you lead a very busy life and sometimes have to work long hours, "sharing" chores is a great way to reconnect with your pet. Just be aware of risks to the bird as you go. You might want to have your bird on your shoulder while you prepare vegetables for stir-fry (your bird will be more than happy to sample things for you), but you'll want to put it back in the cage before you turn on the stove. Always put the bird in a separate room before you take out harsh cleaning supplies, such as bleach or oven cleaner.

Also, be very careful not to forget that the bird is on your shoulder and inadvertently go out or answer the doorbell. It only takes one moment of forgetfulness for a tragedy to occur.

Hanging Out

A tame cockatiel can be like a buddy, and like any good buddy, it enjoys hanging out with you, even if you're not doing anything in particular. They like to perch on your shoulder while you watch TV, share your munchies, listen to you talk, and engage in mutual improvement sessions when you preen each other.

Simply hanging out with your pet cockatiel is probably the best part of owning one. With dogs or cats, it's almost a given that they'll spend time with you, but when a small, trusting little bird sits contentedly with you, letting you touch it and talk to it contrary to whatever wild instincts would ordinarily make it flee from you, you are reminded what a privilege it is to have a tame pet bird.

Chapter Seven

Cockatiel Care and Maintenance

In a lot of ways, cockatiels are low maintenance—which isn't the same as "no maintenance." A clean cage, a little food and water, and some daily quality time with you are all vital to keeping your cockatiel happy and healthy. Here are a few other things about cockatiels that you'll need to know.

Basic Care

Wing Clipping

A wing clip is when the long primary feathers on each wing are cut with a pair of scissors so that the bird is unable to gain or maintain altitude when it tries to fly. Because there are no nerves in a fully grown-in feather, it doesn't hurt the bird, although it may squawk in indignation when the wing is extended so the feathers can be cut. It's similar to when a person gets a haircut, not only because it's painless but because it's not permanent. Just as your hair will continue to grow after it's cut, the feather will eventually fall out when the bird molts and a new one will grow in its place. Unless they're cut, these new feathers will grow to be just as long as a normal primary feather, and the bird will eventually regain its ability to fly.

It's also important to note that, just because a bird's wings are clipped, it doesn't mean it's safe to take it out of doors. Because of the aerodynamic design of a bird's wing, sometimes all it takes is a good wind catching the bird just the wrong way, and the bird will take off and fly a considerable distance in spite of the clipped wings. In addition, because the bird may be able to fly on just one or two primary feathers, it could very possibly take off and fly away before all of the clipped feathers have been molted and replaced. Clip the wings as a training aide and as a way of decreasing the likelihood of the bird escaping, but do not depend on it as a way of keeping your bird safe.

The layers of feathers provide a natural guide of where it's safe to cut when trimming the wing, although the coloring of the feathers may differ from the colors shown in this illustration.

How to Clip Your Cockatiel's Wings

If you're nervous (and even if you're not), it's generally a good idea to ask the person who sells you your cockatiel how to clip its wings. Seeing somebody do it in person gave me the confidence to try it myself because I knew just how to hold the bird, where to cut, and that it really was a painless procedure. But in the event that you don't have anyone to demonstrate, or if you want step-by-step directions to make sure you're doing it right, here's a simple guide to wing trimming.

If you're a novice, the easiest thing to do is to have someone else hold the bird while you wield the scissors. Be sure not to hold the bird too tightly—just tightly enough to

restrain it. Because cockatiels don't have a diaphragm to control their breathing, they need to be able to expand and contract their chest muscles in order to push the air in and out of their lungs. If you hold the bird too tightly, the chest muscles can't expand and the bird won't be able to breathe.

If the bird struggles and tries to bite when you go to pick it up, it may be helpful to drape a small towel over the bird, covering the bird's head and body. Once your bird is covered, pick it up and carefully peel the towel back to reveal the first wing. Be careful to pull the wing away from the body the same way that it unfolds naturally, out to the side rather than up. I've had birds that are calm enough that I can trim their wings by myself without the use of the towel, but if it's your first wing trim, you'll probably want to use the towel just to make sure you don't get bitten.

Once the wing is extended, you'll see that the top edge is smooth and slightly bent, while the bottom is made up of the rounded edges of feathers that get longer the farther they are from the bird's body. The bones in the wing run along the smooth top edge—under no circum-

stances do you want to make a cut here. You'll note that, as you look down from above, you see several layers of feather. The layers of short feathers closest to the top edge of the wing are called the secondaries; the longer feathers that grow out from underneath the secondaries are called the primaries. The primaries are needed for the bird to gain and maintain altitude. These are the ones you need to clip to keep the bird from flying.

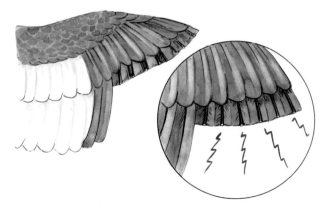

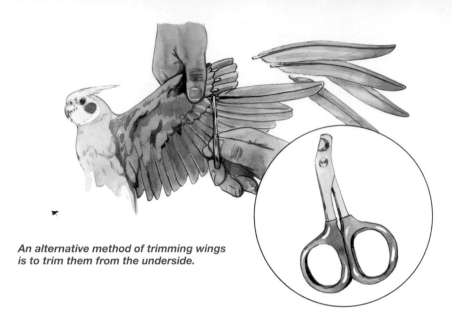

An alternative method of trimming wings is to trim them from the underside.

Using a sharp pair of scissors, cut the eight to ten primary feathers farthest from the body, just below the rounded edges of the secondaries farthest from the edge of the wing. If you've done this correctly, when you look at the bird from behind with its wings closed, you'll see the primaries extending from underneath the wing on the unclipped side, but they won't be visible on the clipped side. Repeat the process on the opposite wing.

Once you've finished clipping the second wing, encourage the bird to fly in order to see how effective the clip was. A properly done clip will let the bird achieve forward motion, but not gain altitude or achieve sustained flight. You don't want the bird to drop like a stone when it tries to fly, but rather, to be

Although, trimming this way eliminates the possibility of using the edge of the secondary feathers as a guide of where to cut and is not recommended for a first-time wing trimmer.

able to glide to the ground safely. If the cockatiel is still able to fly, try re-clipping each wing to take off the bottoms of a couple more primary feathers, or trim a little closer to the secondaries—some cockatiels manage to be really tenacious when it comes to flying even after their wings are clipped.

Nail Clipping

Like people's, a cockatiel's toe-nails grow constantly and need an occasional trimming. A healthy length for a cockatiel's nails is when the tip of the nail just touches the floor of the cage when the bird stands on a flat surface. If the toe is pushed upward to accommodate the length of the nail, it's past time to trim the nails. If you find that the nails are so sharp that it hurts when the bird perches on you, you may also want to trim the tip of the nail straight across, blunting the tip.

As with wing clips, it's generally helpful to watch someone else clip your cockatiel's toenails before you attempt it yourself. Like a wing clip, a nail clip is most easily achieved when you have someone else to hold the bird for you. Wrapping the bird in a small towel and holding it so that only the foot you're working on is exposed is the easiest way to avoid being bitten. The nails can be clipped with a nail clipper designed for a human baby, with nail scissors, or with specially designed clippers for birds or cats that are available at pet stores. Regular-sized human nail clippers can also be used, but their size can make it difficult to see what you're doing.

Cockatiels' nails have a blood vessel called the quick that runs down through the center of the nail. This quick is fairly easy to see in light-colored mutations such as luti-nos, which have pink feet and translucent nails, but is much harder to discern in gray-footed mutations that have dark-colored toenails. You want to avoid clipping so closely that you cut the quick—doing so will result in bleeding, hurt the bird, and make a bloody mess. If you can't see the quick, be very conservative in your nail clipping. You want to clip the nail just enough that the toe lies flat when the tip of the nail is in contact with the floor.

If you do happen to nick the quick when you clip your cockatiel's toe-nails, the nail will immediately start to bleed. Don't panic. A slight nick will stop after just a few drops of blood have fallen. If the nail bleeds more than this, try to stop the bleeding yourself. Styptic sticks, available at many pet supply stores, can be used and should be a part of any good cockatiel first aid kit. If you find your-self with a heavily bleeding nail and no styptic stick, try to dip the bleed-ing tip in corn starch or flour to help staunch the flow of the blood and to encourage clotting. If neither of these work, take the bird to the nearest veterinarian as quickly as possible.

Bathing

Bathing your cockatiel is a healthy thing to do. Not only will it

Sometimes just the sound of running water will cause a cockatiel to get into a bathing position.

help keep your bird clean, but it will improve the health of the feathers and help to keep the dander down.

Sometimes you get birds who love to bathe—they may even try splashing themselves clean in your drink—while others are a bit more reluctant to get wet. Although there are commercially made cockatiel baths available, a pie pan full of water serves just as well, offering a shallow body of water for the bird to wade and splash in. Reluctant cockatiels can be encouraged to bathe by seeing their owners splashing the water with their fingers.

If your cockatiel is still reluctant to take a bath, you can give it a shower by using a plant mister or a spray bottle set on "mist." Using water that is more or less room temperature, aim the mister over the bird's head so that the water falls down over the bird as a gentle rain would. Avoid squirting the water directly at the bird. You wouldn't enjoy it and neither will your cockatiel.

Some cockatiels will squawk and try to get away from the water. This is a typical reaction to any new and unexpected experience. Simply spray the bird until it's wet all over and then let the bird air dry. You might want to bathe the bird less often in cooler weather. My rule of thumb is that if it's warm enough in the house for me

An overgrown beak is frequently a sign of an underlying health problem. Generally speaking, cockatiels' beaks wear down naturally and never need trimming.

to leave my hair wet after washing it, then it's warm enough in the house to bathe the cockatiel.

Some people take their birds into the shower with them, but I don't do this with my cockatiels. The spray from my showerhead is too hard for it to be comfortable or pleasant for the little cockatiel. You'll need to use your own discretion if this is something that you're interested in trying with your bird. It might be best to adjust the spray to its softest setting, if you have an adjustable shower-head. Or, stand holding your bird so that it isn't directly under the spray as it comes out of the showerhead, so that the spray is deflected off your body and onto the bird.

Once the bird gets used to the idea of bathing, it will most likely enjoy it and assume all kinds of interesting positions to let the water seep down between the feathers to reach its skin. A typical cockatiel that's enjoying its bath will lower its head and spread its wings and tail feathers, fluffing out as many of its body feathers as it can. The bird may try to hide its head under one of its wings when this happens, but that doesn't mean it isn't enjoying itself—it's just trying to keep the water out of its eyes!

Beak Care

A normal cockatiel's beak will be worn down through daily use and should never need to be trimmed. An overly long beak can be a sign of illness and malnutrition and you should take your bird to the veterinarian to determine the cause.

Taming, Training, and Tricks

Taming

Although it's easiest to begin with a pet cockatiel that's already tame, that's not always possible. Luckily, cockatiels are social birds who really want a flock to belong to, and in the absence of other birds, they will look to humans to form the rest of the flock. It may take time and patience, but a tame cockatiel is much happier than one that is fearful and feels isolated. In the end, taming is better for both you and your bird.

The first step in training your bird is to gain its trust. Make sure that the bird is located in a place where it can see you and the other members of

your household throughout most of the day. Familiarity becomes its own form of reassurance; the bird is much less likely to be afraid of you if it sees you often and begins to realize that you do not pose a threat to it.

Even with a tame bird, I recommend not trying to handle it for the first 24 to 48 hours in order to give it a chance to observe its new surroundings and begin to feel settled. With an untamed bird, this is even more important; allowing a longer period before you begin to attempt to befriend it is sometimes advisable.

If it's at all possible, ask the person you get the bird from, or your avian veterinarian during your first checkup, to trim the bird's wings for you so that it can't fly. This will make taming the bird exponentially easier because you won't constantly have to chase

the bird around the house in order to retrieve it, making you appear predator-like to the bird. It's also a good idea because cockatiels are fast and retrieving one that doesn't want to be retrieved can be a major hassle. If you do have to retrieve an untamed bird, don't be tempted to use a net to scoop the bird up in flight; you'll risk hurting one of its delicate wings or hitting the bird with the rim of the net, neither of which will help you in your quest to tame it. The safest way to retrieve a loose bird that doesn't want to be retrieved is to wait until the bird lands, then toss a towel over it. It won't be able to take off and you'll be able to see the outline of the bird and pick it up safely without getting bit in the process.

Try to be conscious of how you act in front of the bird. Don't raise your voice or discipline your kids in front of it. Do take a minute or two to talk to it and tell it how pretty it is before you reach into the cage to begin feeding and watering.

One mistake that most people make when they're interacting with a strange or shy bird is to stare at it. In the wild, if a predator is stalking an animal, it keeps its eye on its prey the entire time. For this reason, being stared at makes the bird think of danger on an instinctual level and gives it the impulse to flee. Something similar happens with humans, and that's why people are uncomfortable being stared at. Unfortunately, your impulse is to keep your gaze fixed on your new cockatiel, making it want to try to get away from you. When you talk to your bird, glance away every few seconds or exaggerate when you blink, keeping your eyes closed for a second or two longer than you usually would. Sometimes a cockatiel will blink back at you, a sort of "I'm okay; you're okay" reassurance. Not only does it recognize that you're not a predator, but it's letting you know that it doesn't see any threats either. If it does this, it's a good sign for your relationship. If you notice your bird closing its eyes or blinking obviously at you, the correct response is to return this reassurance and blink back at it. It's a first step in building a bond between you.

Make an effort to spend quiet time together. Sit near the bird while you read or engage in some other quiet activity, such as knitting or doing a puzzle. Talk to the bird softly as you do, maybe even reading to it or singing or whistling a favorite song.

Eating in front of your cockatiel is a great way of attracting its attention, and is the next step in the taming process. Be sure to let it see how much you like whatever you're eating, then offer it some through the bars. Don't expect the bird to eagerly come take the food from your hand at first. You could simply say "Want some?" and then wedge a bit of banana or a nacho chip between the bars of the cage for the bird to sample when it works up the courage. Make sure that whatever food you're using as "bait" the bird only gets directly from you. Don't slip a handful of the food you're sharing into its dish when you have to leave—this food should be a special treat and should only come from you. Tortilla chips work especially well for this because not only do most cockatiels seem to love corn, but the large size of the chip will allow a lot of space between your fingers and the edge of the food that the cockatiel will be tasting, lessening the chance that you'll get bit during the process.

If the bird ignores the food you slip between the bars, don't assume that it doesn't like it. It may take a while for the bird to work up enough courage to approach the bars when the food is placed between them. Taming a bird can be a long, sometimes frustrating process, but be patient—the end result will be that much more satisfying because of the amount of effort you put into it.

does this, repeat the process for a few days in a row to make sure the bird is comfortable doing it. If it stands or perches on your hand in order to get at the food, that's great; just keep still and let the bird eat from there. Try not to move your hand until you need to (if it gets to be too uncomfortable or you have to leave), or the bird decides to get off on its own.

The next step is to open the cage door but hold the food a little farther back, so that the bird has to perch on the open doorway to be able to reach it. This stage can be relatively short, since you are now gaining the bird's trust. Over the next day or two, start to hold the food farther out, so that you have to put your free hand between the cage door and the food in order to provide a "step" for the bird to reach the treat. If it wants to get to the treat, it will have to perch on your hand outside the cage to do it.

Once the bird finishes the treat, you can offer it another or give it the chance to return to the cage. You've just hit a major milestone in your relationship and will soon reach the point where the cockatiel will actually rush to the cage door as soon as it's opened and willingly hop on your hand. Soon you can try nudging the bird gently on the chest, just in front of the legs, and saying "Up," teaching it its very first trick—stepping up on command.

The final step is to carefully reach up and see if your cockatiel will let you preen it, touching its head, rub-

Once the bird takes the food from between the bars a few days in a row, it's time to raise the stakes a little and hold onto the other end of the treat once you slip it between the bars, so that the cockatiel has to approach your hand in order to get it. Again, once this has been achieved, repeat the process for a few days so that the bird becomes quite comfortable approaching your hand. Don't be tempted to think, "Okay, he took it while I was holding it; it's time to move on to the next step." That kind of thinking can rush things and actually set the taming process back.

Once you have the bird taking food from your hand through the bars, the next step is to open the cage door and to offer the favored treat from there. Again, once the bird

bing its cheek spots, and scratching its head and neck. The bird may eventually want to reciprocate, preening your hair or trying to nibble off your freckles. At that point, you can safely say that your cockatiel is "tame."

Simple Tricks

Cockatiels, being intelligent animals, can be taught to do simple tricks. This can be achieved through a combination of reinforcing their natural tendencies and teaching them to respond to cues from you. Although it's not necessary to teach your bird tricks—cockatiels are perfectly delightful just as they are—if you want to give it a try as a way of spending quality time with your bird, go ahead. Just remember that you want these learning experiences to be pleasant and fun for both of you, and that means never punishing or scolding your bird for not responding the way you want it to. Chances are that the bird didn't understand what you wanted it to do, and wouldn't understand why you imposed a negative consequence. In general, a negative consequence for your cockatiel should never be anything stronger than being returned to its cage and deprived of your attention for a time.

Stepping up: The most important single "trick" you can teach your cockatiel is how to step up onto your hand on command. This is important not just because it makes your relationship easier, but it can help to calm and focus the bird in an emergency.

Many cockatiels will come to you already knowing how to do this, particularly if they were hand-fed or well socialized as youngsters. All this "trick" involves is simply placing the side of your hand against the bird's belly just in front of the legs, giving a gentle nudge and telling the bird to step onto your hand. The actual words you use are up to you, but most people use some variation of "Up" or "Step up." Whatever words you choose will work as long as you use them consistently every time you do it. "Let's go," "Come on," or even "Time to play!" will all work.

When the bird successfully steps up on command, reward it with praise, a treat, or by scratching its head. Cockatiels love high-pitched, enthusiastic voices, no matter how cheesy you might feel using them (in fact, the cheesier I sound, the better they seem to like it). Eventually the bird will come to associate stepping up with spending quality time with you, and that will be its own reward, although a friendly head rub will always be appreciated.

If a bird is slow to respond to a command, or starts to act belligerently, you can remind it of your authority by asking it repeatedly to step up from one hand to the other, reinforcing your position as the "top bird."

Potty Training

Many people are surprised to learn that you can potty train a cockatiel. In fact, many kinds of pet birds can be trained to relieve themselves on command or in a particular location. To begin with, though, it's the owner who needs to be trained as much as the bird.

It's possible to recognize that a bird is about to relieve itself. The body tenses slightly and the bird more or less "backs up" where it stands, so that when it lets loose, the poop falls down to the ground or cage floor rather than soiling the branch on which it is standing. In fact, if you can learn to recognize this tensing and backing up, it's possible to move a bird that's sitting on your hand away from your body before it poops, keeping the mess from falling on your clothing.

To actually potty train a bird to go on command is more difficult. First, whenever you notice the physical signs that your bird is about to relieve itself, say whatever words you want to use to signal the bird to go. The words themselves don't matter, as long as you use them consistently. "Go potty" is a frequent choice, although I have one acquaintance who, last I heard, was using the phrase "Bombs away!" to get his bird to go on command (as a guy, he didn't think saying "Go potty" was suitable for a male in his prime). Every time you see the bird tense and begin to back up, say whatever words you choose so that the bird begins to associate the command with the action.

You'll also need to figure out where you want the bird to relieve itself, since the location will also be part of the cue you use. I've only tried potty training one of my cockatiels, a hen who frequently laid eggs. When they're getting ready to lay eggs or when they have chicks, hens will "hold it in" for long periods of time; then they move some distance away from the nest and let loose a pile of droppings of epic proportions. I got tired of cleaning monster piles of poop off my kitchen floor, and so I decided to train her to go in the dirt of my biggest potted plant, where I just had to turn the dirt over to dispose of the mess.

Some people hold the bird over a newspaper or paper towels for easier cleanup. I've even seen people who actually hold the bird perched on one hand and a folded square of paper towel under the bird's vent to catch the droppings; they can give the command wherever they happen to be, which is very convenient if you take your bird different places with you, such as on vacation or to work. Holding the bird directly over the toilet is not a good idea, as you don't want your bird frequenting the bathroom. Unsupervised birds have been known to fall into open toilet bowls and drown, so it's best to keep your cockatiel out of the bathroom entirely.

The next step is a bit tricky. Assuming your bird is fairly regular in its bodily functions, time the intervals between so that you can predict when the next event will occur. For example, if your bird relieves itself approximately every twelve minutes, start timing from the moment it poops, and eleven minutes later, move your bird onto your hand, place it where you want it to go, and start giving the verbal cue. When the bird successfully poops, reward it with praise, head scratches, and perhaps a small treat. Do this over and over again and, theoretically, your bird will get the idea and associate the location, the command, and the action, so that it goes on command.

Talking

Talking is sort of an iffy proposition. Theoretically, any cockatiel can talk, but most don't. Think of it in human terms: Most people are physically able to walk on their hands, juggle, or play the piano, but most never do. The physical equipment is there, but that doesn't necessarily mean it's going to happen. And like the skills mentioned above, different cockatiels will have different levels of success when it comes to talking. It might happen or it might not; you just have to accept your bird, whatever its abilities.

There are several recorded programs available that are intended to help your bird learn to talk. They include tapes, CDs, and DVDs that repeat the same words and phrases over and over so that the bird will learn them without you repeating things over and over until you feel a bit like a parrot yourself. Although these might be effective, they will never be as engaging for the bird as when you talk to it. The repetitive sounds eventually become background noise and lose the bird's interest.

To teach your bird to talk, first figure out what it is you want it to say. Try to remember that your bird doesn't understand what it's saying at first, and try to come up with a phrase that makes sense if the bird is the one saying it. A friend wanted to teach her cockatiel, Charlie, to say "Hello," and so several times a day she'd say "Hello, Charlie!" Now she's greeted every morning when she gets up by the cheerful sound of Charlie wishing himself a good morning. This same friend's budgie also tells her "You're a damned cute bird!" which, while pretty funny, isn't quite what she'd had in mind.

Pick something that's simple and short, no more than a few syllables long. It's best if you have a word or phrase that comes out with a fair amount of enthusiasm, like "Hello!" or "Peekaboo!" Speak clearly and enthusiastically. An emphatic voice is much more likely to catch the cockatiel's attention and make it interested enough to want to try to copy it.

It's said that males that are raised by hand away from other birds are the most likely to talk. This may or may not be true. Certainly, male cockatiels are more likely to speak than females.

It's not a good idea to teach your bird to whistle before you try to teach it to talk; whistling comes much easier and once they master it, cockatiels seem content to communicate by whistling rather than speaking. I've heard that they are more likely to imitate a female voice than a male's,

Although cockatiels rarely talk, the males can be excellent at whistling.

phones, beeping microwaves, or chiming video games. One of my birds began his life in a household where the lady also bred show dogs, and as a result we've lived with the sound of a small, yappy dog for several years now, even though we don't own a dog ourselves.

Whistling

Whistling is closer to a cockatiel's natural voice than human speech is, and consequently, cockatiels pick up whistling much faster than speaking. In many cases, they learn it from the television (frequently the old "Andy Griffith Show Theme") or the radio (rifts from "Sittin' on the Dock of the Bay" and "Don't Worry, Be Happy"). If you leave the TV or radio on while you're at work, there's no telling what your cockatiel might pick up from it.

As with talking, males are much more likely to pick up a repertoire of whistled songs than females. Some cockatiels are very proficient whistlers while others are not so good. We thought it would be cute to teach our first cockatiel, Cookie, how to whistle the *Sesame Street* song "C is for Cookie"—a dozen years later, he's got the first five notes perfectly, but after that he's never done the song the same way twice. But that's okay; his messed-up version of his personal theme song is just one more endearing part of life with Cookie!

but since I live in a household full of women, I can't attest to that. They may also be more likely to learn words that end with a vowel sound rather than a consonant.

It's also worth noting that cock-atiels have been known to imitate sounds other than speech. If there are other birds within earshot, it's highly likely that your cockatiel may pick up their calls, even if the other bird isn't a cockatiel. Several of mine do excellent budgie imitations. They may also learn to imitate ringing

Chapter Eight
Behavior

Owning a pet cockatiel is similar to having a toddler. You new pet will need affection, interaction—and a whole lot of supervision. Like any two year old, you will encounter behaviors that need to be modified. Biting, noise, and getting into things that are potentially dangerous are all problems that cockatiel owners can encounter. This chapter will discuss some of these behaviors and suggest ways of dealing with them.

Bad Behaviors

One of the keys to fixing bad behaviors in birds is to try to figure out their causes, particularly if the bad behavior is a recent development. First, look for patterns—does the bird scream or bite whenever you reach in to pick it up? A visit to the veterinarian may be in order to rule out medical causes, since a painful but undetected medical condition such as a broken bone would certainly explain the changes in behavior.

Do the undesirable behaviors center on just one member of the household? If so, look for what it is about this person that might be setting the bird off. Assuming that he or she is always gentle and careful with the bird rather than abusive, it's possible that the bird has seen the person doing something that upset it. Changes in a trusted person's appearance can sometimes cause the bird to react differently. It may not quite be able to recognize you with a new haircut or glasses, and may feel stressed and suspicious because you seem familiar and strange at the same time. Bright-red nail polish is one frequently overlooked cause to changes in a cockatiel's behavior. Because cockatiels can see colors, deep-red nails remind them on some level of bloody claws reaching toward them.

The time of day when undesirable behaviors occur can also provide a clue to their cause. Does the bird always scream at eight thirty in the morning? Maybe it's reacting to the sound of neighborhood children congregating at the bus stop just outside. Does it bite you whenever the person you're dating comes over? Bonded birds will sometimes bite each other when they want their loved one to flee—a very useful thing in the wild when a predator is sighted, but extremely annoying when the jealous bird wants you to flee from your significant other.

One quick fix that's worth trying is to make sure your bird's cage and play stands are low enough that your bird is no higher than your eye level. According to one school of thought, wild birds roost according to a hierarchy of rank, and the top birds occupy the highest spots in the tree. Therefore, a bird that looks down on you will come to think of itself as your superior and may begin to act up, refusing to step up on command, biting, and making a general nuisance of itself. This wasn't always the cause of behavior problems, but it's something to consider when these issues present themselves. If you can identify the cause of an undesirable behavior, it's that much easier to correct it. If you can't identify the cause and none of the suggestions below help, try seeking out a behavioral consultant, a sort of psychotherapist for birds. Behavioral consultants, who can be found through advertisements in bird magazines or online, will consult with you for a fee either in person, online, or by phone about how to best modify your cockatiel's undesirable behaviors.

Biting

Since they don't have hands, it's only natural that cockatiels explore things with their mouths. As a general rule, these explorations are lim-

How to Discipline Your Cockatiel

It's extremely important to remember that you should never try to modify a cockatiel's behavior by "punishing" it. *Never* yell at the bird, hit it, shake it, bang on the cage roof, or do anything that may physically harm or emotionally damage your bird. Punishment won't work because the cockatiel will not understand why you are punishing it. Furthermore, any actions that you take that inspire fear in the bird will negatively impact your relationship. You can't have a loving pet if that pet is afraid of you. The worse consequence for any bad behavior should be to return your cockatiel to its cage and remove yourself from the room. These "time-outs" will give both of you a chance to calm down and regroup without any long-term repercussions.

ited to nibbles and licks, which are either endearing or annoying, depending on your tolerance level. In addition, some things act like magnets for a nibbling cockatiel. Glasses, freckles, moles, and jewelry all make irresistible targets for curious cockatiels.

A nibbling cockatiel can sometimes be deterred by giving the surface it's standing on a small shake—not hard, but just enough to divert its attention to keeping its bal-

ance. If that fails, a distraction may be in order; give the bird a treat, move it to stand on the other hand or shoulder, or try to coax it into whistling instead of nibbling. If the cockatiel persists in going after the same thing time and time again, a brief return to the cage may be in order to get the bird's mind off the object of its obsession.

Biting is much more serious. Although their beaks are relatively small, they can still inflict a painful bite and, if they hit a particularly vulnerable spot, may even draw blood. As with other behavioral issues, it's best if you can determine the cause of the bird's biting so that you can eliminate the problem at the source. Some possible causes are mentioned above.

If a bird bites because it doesn't want to be taken out of the cage, there are a couple of things you can try. First, leave the cage door open and offer a treat just outside the door to see if the bird will come out on its own. Cockatiels are generally not territorial when it comes to their cages, but it is possible. If this is the case, the bird may be easier to handle once it's away from the cage; you'll simply need to let the bird come out on its own.

If you have a bird that truly is afraid of hands, you might look into handheld perches, which are usually made of wood and shaped like a "T." The owner holds the long part of the T and nudges the bird's chest just in front of its legs with the top of the T in order to coax it into stepping onto the crossbar. Some of these handheld perches even come with a sheet of Plexiglas just above where your hand goes in order to shield you from possible bites. These can be used indefinitely or until the cockatiel becomes comfortable enough for you to pick it up without the perch.

Birds who are habitual biters can be discouraged by a product that has a nasty, bitter taste. These products come in a liquid form and are available at many pet supply stores. You simply rub some on your hands before you pick up the bird, and if the cockatiel does bite, it will be repelled by the taste. Because this type of product is used for other types of biting pets as well as for birds, it may not be carried with the bird supplies, and you may have to ask the clerk if the store carries it. If you are using an online pet supply catalog, it's fre-

quently listed with ferret supplies. This type of product can also be used to discourage unwanted obsessive nibbling, such as if your cockatiel persistently picks at your freckles or tries to remove your mole.

It's also possible that your tame, beloved pet cockatiel will suddenly bite you hard and without warning in the presence of another person. This seems to be a completely unprovoked attack, but in the cockatiel's mind, it makes perfect sense. In the wild, if a cockatiel sees what it perceives as a threat, such as a predator, it will frequently bite its mate hard to get her to flee the area. This may be the case with your bird—it either views the new arrival as a potential threat to your safety or as a rival for your affections, and so it will try to get you to quickly leave the area with an unexpected bite. In this case, the best course of action is to return your bird to its cage (and preferably out of sight of your guest) until the visit is over.

Screaming

The noise factor in birds is pretty much a matter of tolerance. Compared to other kinds of parrots, cockatiels are relatively quiet. That said, I have neighbors who live about 50 feet away and I can hear their cockatiel when it starts to make its flock call. A flock call is the loud sound that a bird makes when it wants to locate other members of its flock (including humans) when they're out of sight. It's normally the loudest sound a cockatiel makes, but every now and then, you'll find a bird that's a real screamer.

The first thing to consider when a bird begins to scream is whether or not the bird is injured. Bruises and broken bones may not be visible to you, the owner, but they are certainly painful to the bird and may account for sudden and persistent screaming. If your normally complacent cockatiel suddenly starts shrieking, particularly when it moves or when you try to get it to step up onto your hand, you should immediately suspect an injury and contact your avian veterinarian as soon as possible.

There are several tricks you can try if you have a cockatiel that turns out to be a screamer. Again, if you can determine a cause for the screaming, it will be much easier to figure out a solution.

First of all, is the bird getting 10 to 12 hours a night of uninterrupted sleep in a quiet, dark room? A tired bird is a cranky bird, and a cranky bird is more likely to act out. If your bird is getting less "in bed" time than recommended, either move it into a quiet, darkened room at dusk or cover the cage where it stands.

Secondly, check the volume level in your house. The bird wants to be heard by you when it vocalizes, and if there's a lot of competing noise, the bird will try to make itself louder in order to be heard. Competing noises include the sounds of the television, music, children, the dishwasher, any small appliance, or even another pet, such as a bird or a barking dog.

If you're loud, you can actually teach your bird to be loud. This includes the way you respond to your bird screaming. If you yell at the bird when it's making a lot of noise, instead of understanding that you're upset, your bird will take your response as a sound of approval and will yell back at you, thinking that it's a bonding activity. Your bird will think, "Mom or Dad is being noisy; I can do that, too!" Some birds may actually come to enjoy yelling in order to see your response. They learn that if they yell, they get your attention. It can become almost like a game to them.

The key in this case is not to give the bird a payoff in the way you respond to its vocalizing. Don't raise your voice. Don't respond with anger. Don't do anything that will encourage the bird to keep screaming. Sometimes the solution is as simple as turning and walking out of the room, and not coming back until the bird is quiet again. When you do return, praise it lavishly, scratch its head, and tell it how much you like it when it's a nice, quiet bird. If it starts to rev up in your presence, leave the room again with a minimum of fuss.

Some cockatiels will vocalize when they are lonely. They don't see you, and they want to know that you're still in the vicinity and that you're okay. Calling out "I'm right here" may be enough to reassure your bird to the point that it stops yelling for you. Some cockatiels, particularly young ones, experience a sort of separation anxiety and will start to call as soon as they see you leave the room. In this case, try draping a sheet or a towel over the side of the cage that faces the door and quietly tiptoe out. If the bird doesn't see you leave, it can be tricked into thinking that you're still there, just behind the curtain. As the bird gets older and more secure that it's not being abandoned, you can usually dispose of the covering.

It's generally not a good idea to get into the habit of covering the entire cage when the bird gets noisy, although this will frequently stop the vocalizing, because it's too easy to forget about it and leave the bird in darkened isolation for long periods of time. But in an extreme situation, such as when you need to take an important phone call and the bird is so loud that you can't hear, covering the cage for the duration of the call may be the best solution.

Some cockatiels will get loud trying to attract your attention when you're in the same room with them. If this is the case, try whispering to them in reply, speaking so quietly that the bird has to stop the noise it's making in order to hear what you're saying. This not only gets the bird to stop its vocalizing in order to listen to you, but also models how to communicate quietly, so that your bird may eventually realize that it doesn't have to be loud in order to be heard.

Some people suggest that a bird vocalizes because it's lonely, and they recommend that you acquire a second bird in order to satisfy the first bird's need for a companion. While this may be the case if you are busy and work long hours, if your bird is making noise because it knows you're in the house and wants your attention, getting a second bird may not appease it, and you could end up with two loud birds instead.

Plucking

Cockatiels aren't so high strung that they tend to pull out their own feathers or, worse, pick at their skin to the point where they make themselves bleed, but it does occasionally happen. Some birds will pick at just a particular patch on their bodies, while others will eventually pull off every feather they can reach, leaving them looking something like a gray roasting chicken with a feathered head. In other cases, it's not the bird itself that's pulling out its feathers, but a companion bird that is overly enthusiastic when it comes to preening. You can tell if it's the bird itself or the companion based on whether or not the head is plucked—a cockatiel can't reach to pluck its own head. But remember, some mutations of cockatiels, such as lutinos, have a genetic defect that leaves some of them with a large bald patch just behind the crest. In this case, the problem isn't plucking, and there's no solution: Your bird will naturally have a bald patch all its life, and you just have to love it the way it is.

If you're not sure who's doing the plucking, just watch for a while. Eventually you should see the culprit in action. If the companion bird is doing the plucking, separate them. You'll have to take over preening the unreachable areas when the feathers grow back in, but at least you're bird won't be bald.

Feather plucking is not the same as molting. As birds age, their feathers naturally fall out and new feathers grow in to replace them, much the same way that a person's hairs fall out and are replaced by new ones. Some birds molt gradually while others seem to shed a lot of feathers all at once. It used to look like a bird exploded every time one of my lutinos shook because so many feathers would seem to fly off of her at once. The difference between plucking and molting is that a bird molts all over its body, not just in one patch; a bare patch means plucking while the loss of a few feathers here and there is just a regular molt. When a bird preens itself, it will occasionally find a loose, about-to-be-molted feather, and you may well see your bird pull out that feather with its mouth, chew on it for a bit, and then drop it. However, that's still part of regular molting, not to be confused with plucking.

The first thing to do when your bird is plucking is to make sure that there's no physical cause for the bird to be pulling its feathers out. Although birds don't host fleas the way dogs and cats do, they can be infested with mites. Mites are very small insects that bite the bird in order to feed on its blood. Nearly incessant scratching, crying out as if in pain for no apparent reason, and

A cockatiel will preen every feather it can reach on a daily basis.

pulling out feathers by the beakful are all signs that you may have a problem with mites. To determine whether or not mites are the problem, remove all of the cage bedding just before bed and replace it with white paper towels. Instead of the usual cage cover, drape the cage with a plain white towel or sheet. Turn out the light and go to bed as usual, but first thing in the morning, examine the paper towels and cage covering for small, red dots—these are the mites, which are more active at night than during the day. If you don't see any mites, other possible causes for the itching and plucking should be pursued. It could be an indication of giardia (a parasite that infects the bird after being ingested through contact with feces, spoiled food, or contaminated water) or an allergic reaction.

There are several possible causes for plucking, including malnutrition, mites, illness, and behavioral issues.

If you find that your bird does have mites, you can either consult your veterinarian or try a commercially available mite spray to get rid of them. Be sure to follow the directions on the bottle and to spray the cage and its surroundings as well as the cockatiel to prevent reinfestation. It's not a good idea to spray your bird, with mite spray "just in case" or as a preventive measure. If your bird comes to you free of mites, is never exposed to another bird, and never spends any time outdoors, it is extremely unlikely that it will ever come into contact with mites. The spray is a mild pesticide that could

have residual effects, so you don't want to expose your bird to it unless you're certain it's necessary.

The second possible cause of feather plucking is a health issue, which can only be properly diagnosed by your veterinarian. Nutritional deficiencies can cause feathers to fall out, as can certain diseases. Although psittacine beak and feather disease is frequently mentioned as a possible cause of feather loss among parrots, some recent studies suggest that cockatiels simply don't get this condition. If you're sure your bird is plucking, make an appointment to see your veterinarian as soon as possible to rule out physical causes.

The third possible cause of feather plucking in cockatiels is the most difficult to remedy: when the bird starts to pluck for behavioral reasons. Birds can start to pluck their feathers as a response to extreme stress, similar to the way some people might chew their nails, or as a result of neglect (they start to pull out their own feathers simply for the stimulation it provides). If it goes on for too long, plucking becomes an ingrained habit that's extremely difficult to break.

Just like with other behavioral problems, the first step is to try to determine why the bird plucks. Look honestly at how much time you spend interacting with your cockatiel. Do you talk to it and take it out for daily interaction, or are you only paying attention to it long enough to put food and water in its dishes once a day? If you realize that you are not able to give the bird the time and attention it needs, it may be a sign that it's time to give up the bird to a better home.

If you suspect that your bird is plucking because of a lack of attention on your part, make an effort to lavish more attention on it. Start by changing the toys in your bird's cage to give it something more interesting to look at and play with. Keep your bird in the same room with you as much as possible and distract it every time you see it going after its feathers. Give it as much out-of-cage time as you can manage and stimulate it with new experiences, such as feeding it fresh foods that it's never tried before. If you have to leave the house, leave the television or radio on rather than leaving it alone in a silent house. Do everything you can to keep the bird's mind off plucking. It might work or it might not, but it's worth a try.

If you have a good relationship with your cockatiel, look for things that might be stressing the bird. Did you recently move? Do you have a dog or cat that may be terrorizing your cockatiel in your absence? Is there another bird in the room that your cockatiel might be afraid of? Does the bird have a window that gives it a view of something outside that could be stressful? One lady I know thought her bird would enjoy having its cage located so that it could look out the window and see the wild birds that congregated at her bird feeder. She couldn't figure out why her cockatiel would periodically scream and thrash against the sides of the cage, eventually starting to pull out its own feathers, until she happened to be in the room one day and glanced out the window when the bird started to freak out. Not only did the bird have a splendid view of the bird feeder—it had a clear view of the hawk that stood on top of the feeder, calmly munching on a blue jay.

Even if you can identify what's stressing out the bird and remove the stressor, the bird may still continue to pluck. Cockatiels have long memories. If you can't identify the stressors, there are still some things you can do, but either way, getting the bird to stop plucking can be a difficult challenge.

You can try spraying or rubbing something that tastes nasty on the bare patch and surrounding feathers, either one of the products marketed to stop pets from biting or a mixture of mustard and water (but never spray anything onto an open wound). In addition, whenever you catch the cockatiel in the act, try to distract it by calling its name, telling it to stop, picking it up, or handing it a treat or offering it a toy.

For persistent pluckers, a veterinarian can put a cone-shaped collar around the bird's neck so that it can't reach its body with its beak. The veterinarian may also try putting a vest over the bird's body to keep it from being able to pull its feathers. The idea is to break the cycle of plucking long enough for it to cease to be a habit. With any luck, the plucking will stop before the feather follicles are irreparably damaged and the bird becomes permanently denuded of feathers.

Sometimes, intervention comes too late and the damage is irreparable, or nothing you try succeeds in stopping the bird from plucking. In these cases, you may well end up with a cockatiel that is naked but otherwise healthy, and you just have to learn to accept and love it for the special little nudist that it is.

Night Frights

Like people, cockatiels sometimes wake up in the middle of the night and get scared. The exact cause is debatable—maybe they had a nightmare, maybe some noise or movement in the house woke them suddenly—but for whatever reason, the bird starts screaming and thrashing in the darkness, waking up the entire household and setting off a chain reaction of panic with the other critters in the house.

The best way to deal with night frights is to get up and comfort the bird, taking it out of the cage, talking to it soothingly, and waiting to make sure it is calm before returning it to its cage. It's a good idea to look the bird over as you comfort it, making sure that it didn't break any blood feathers or otherwise hurt itself thrashing in the darkness. When you go to bed, try leaving the light on in the bird's room if possible; the cockatiel will feel much safer if it can see than it will in the darkness. Most of the time, night frights are one-time events and not an ongoing problem.

If night frights persist and occur night after night, there are several things that you can try to alleviate the problem. First, make a note of just what time the episodes occur and look for a possible cause. Does your neighbor who works the graveyard shift come home at 2:00 in the morning? Do the kids in the neighborhood have to catch the school bus before dawn and congregate just outside your house? Does a distant train blow its whistle as it approaches a street? Is it possible that you have mice that come out at night and startle the bird? If you can find a pattern, you may be able to determine a cause, and thus a way to eliminate the problem. Install a night-light in the bird's room, just as you would for a small child, so that it can see for itself that there's nothing in the room that can harm it. If the bird shares a cage, try putting it by itself at night so that it's not startled in the darkness by its cage mate. A low-playing radio may be used to mask sounds that you don't notice, but which upset your cockatiel. If it continues to be a problem, try moving the bird to a different part of the house to sleep, even if you can't find an obvious cause.

Territorialism

Territorialism is when a bird gets very defensive about a certain location. It may crouch, hiss, lunge, or, in a worst-case scenario, bite at your hand. The cage is usually the center of this aggression, although it can also happen with play stands or with a seemingly random spot outside the cage.

When the problem occurs away from the cage, it often involves a spot that the bird views as a potential nest site. Potential nest sites are usually dark and somewhat enclosed, such as under a dresser, between a row of books and the shelf above them, or in a cabinet or drawer that is left ajar. This sort of behavior is natural and should pass as the bird works its way through its hormonal cycle—think of it as PMS for birds—but be aware that it frequently hits males even harder than females. They feel the urge to mate, and even if there's not another bird around at the moment, they seem to think that it's worth the effort to find and defend a potential nest site, just in case a bird of the opposite sex does magically appear. With females, they may even go so far as to lay eggs in their chosen site, whether or not they've mated. In this case, you can let her defend and incubate them where she sits (although while she's sitting, it's going to seem like your affectionate pet has been replaced by a ferocious harpy). If you leave her to sit with her eggs, she will remain territorial until she decides that they are not going to hatch and abandons them, usually about a month to a month and a half later.

If you want to reclaim the out-of-cage area, remove any eggs to the cage floor and block off access to the area in question. If the bird can't get to the nest site, the bird can't defend it. She may or may not sit on the relocated eggs, but if she does, be aware that she's going to be just as vehement about wanting to protect them in the cage as she was in the original nest site, although she can't charge out to bite you every time you get too close if she's safely locked away in her cage. Simply removing the eggs but allowing her to keep access to her chosen nest site won't stop the defensive behavior—she'll simply lay more eggs there, putting a strain on her body and prolonging your ordeal with her territorial behavior.

A cockatiel that becomes territorial about its cage when it's not a hormonal issue can be more difficult to deal with. Since a bird that is territorial about its cage is frequently a delightful, well-mannered pet when it is away from it, sometimes it's just

easier to open the door and let the bird come out on its own, and to service the cage while the bird is away from it, being held by another member of the household out of view of the cage. This is why, when discussing taming, I did not recommend reaching into the cage but simply letting the bird come to the open doorway on its own. With most cockatiels, you can reach into the cage with no problem; it's just a few headstrong individuals who get belligerent when it comes to defending their turf.

You might also try using more than one cage, shifting the bird from one cage to another when you return it after your interaction sessions, to keep it from developing too great a sense of ownership. I don't have any problems with territorialism with my cockatiels or with my bigger birds, but I do with our resident lovebird. She's fine when she comes out on her own but attacks like a junkyard dog whenever anyone reaches into her cage. If I have to reach in when she's there, I either wear gardening gloves or press a washcloth against the bars at the back of the cage with one hand, and while she's distracted by attacking it, I'll reach in quickly to get what I need to retrieve. She's my daughter's bird and we love her to bits, so this is how we deal with her extreme possessiveness.

Cockatiels may also become territorial about a particular person or object. In the case of an object, such as a toy or a perch, it may be that the bird finds a release for built-up sexual tensions with it (see the section on "tail rubbing" later in this chapter). The simplest solution is to remove the object in question from the cage.

The quirky part about cockatiels is that the person they become fixated on may not be their actual owner or the person who takes care of them. Love is just as fickle in cockatiels as it is in people, and the object of their obsession may not even particularly *like* birds. The trick here is for the less-favored person to work on forging a relationship with the bird separately from the object of its affection. He or she should bring it special treats, take the bird out when the favored person isn't around, preen it, talk to it, and make it feel genuinely liked. Hopefully, the bird will come to like the second person enough that it stops viewing him or her as a threat to its interaction with the favored person.

Reading Cockatiel Body Language

Everyone knows that a dog wags its tail when it's happy and lowers its head and bares its teeth when it feels threatened. Cockatiels will tell you how they're feeling using body language, too—it's just that you're not very adept at interpreting it yet. Here, then, are some of the many gestures, postures, and actions that your cockatiel will employ to tell you what it's feeling.

Crest Up

A cockatiel's crest is like a barometer for its mood. The crest of feathers on top of the head normally stands at about a 75-degree angle. This means that the cockatiel is feeling comfortable and relaxed. When something exciting happens, the crest pops upright, almost perpendicular to the head, indicating interest, happiness, and, perhaps, surprise. You'll probably notice that this happens a lot when you first enter the room in the morning or when you come home from work; it means that your cockatiel is happy to see you.

Crest Down

If a crest up is a sign of happiness and excitement, then a crest that is lowered is a sign of fear or aggression. Be careful when you approach a bird in this position, particularly if the lowered crest is accompanied by a gaping beak—a clear warning that the bird does not want to be handled.

Bowing Down

New cockatiel owners are frequently puzzled by the bowing position that their cockatiels assume when they're interacting. The bird will lower its head so that its body is almost parallel to the floor and its forehead is practically touching the ground. This is an invitation—your

The position of this bird's bowed head tells the owner that it wants its head and neck scratched.

The lowered crest and body position indicate that the lutino is being submissive toward the normal gray, possibly begging for food.

cockatiel is asking you to preen its head and neck. The appropriate response is to oblige it with friendly scratching.

The Crouch

The crouch position is assumed by female cockatiels who want to mate. The body is held almost parallel to the floor, but, unlike the bowing position where the head is lowered, the head is held upright. The wings are held away from the body, the tail is lined up with the rest of the bird, and the tail feathers are slightly spread and held up off the ground. This position is frequently accompanied by a high-pitched chanting—the cockatiel version of a love song—and the bird may quiver in excitement.

If you have a male and a female and don't want chicks, it's a really good idea to separate them as soon as you see this posturing. If you don't have a male or another bird, it's entirely possible that your cockatiel is hoping you'll be the one to satisfy it sexually. Needless to say, this isn't going to happen, which may make your bird very frustrated. It may be a good idea to lessen your contact with the bird for a few days until the cockatiel's urges have passed.

This posturing may be followed in a few weeks by signs that your hen is getting ready to lay eggs. You'll notice that, when she's out of the cage, she spends a lot of time checking out small, dark places around the house, such as open drawers, cabinets, and under furniture. She's looking for a suitable nesting site. Just before she lays the eggs, her droppings will become less frequent and positively huge in comparison to the average dropping. When you see these signs, you need to keep a close eye on her—whether she mated or not, she's about to lay eggs.

Tail Rubbing

An elderly lady I know once asked me to come take a look at her bird. He'd started "swinging his tail" back and forth rapidly for several minutes at a time. I stopped by to visit and saw no problem—the bird seemed happy and well cared for, and I didn't notice any strange behaviors. Knowing that birds can be fickle beasts when it comes to doing what you want when there's someone else to see it, I offered to stay for a visit in case the bird started acting strangely.

Partway through a cup of tea, it happened. My friend pointed at the birdcage and exclaimed, "There! That's what he does!" I looked over at the cage and saw what she did: The bird was standing on his perch with his tail swishing back and forth like a pendulum. But I noticed what she'd missed: Not only was the tail swishing, but the bird had his vent area pressed against the perch, so that it rubbed against the hard wooden surface. Her bird was masturbating.

If a crouch is a sign of a sexually ready female, then a male's rubbing of the vent area—the spot underneath the bird just above the tail— against a hard surface is a sign of

sexual frustration. Not all male cockatiels engage in this activity, but those that do may rub against a perch, a toy, or even against their owner's hand. It's as normal for cockatiels as it is for people, although cockatiels are very uninhibited and will perform the act whether or not there's an audience present. Unless you are willing to get the bird a mate, and thus go through the ordeal of having a clutch of eggs, you might try limiting the number of hours a day that the bird is exposed to light in order to fool it into thinking that it's not a good time of year for breeding (eight to ten hours a day), but there's really nothing you can do to curb this activity. The bird will feel better for having found an outlet for his frustrations, and you can safely ignore it.

If, however, your bird engages in this activity in front of guests, and you are not comfortable telling them the truth about what he's up to, you can always tell them what I told my elderly friend. Because she was older and had more delicate sensibilities, I thought that she might be offended if I told her the truth, so thinking fast, I blurted out, "He's polishing his perch!"

It wasn't quite the truth, but it satisfied her curiosity and alleviated any concerns that something was wrong with her beloved pet. She's happy; the bird is happy. And she's convinced that she has the cleverest and neatest cockatiel that ever lived.

Standing Tall and Thin

A cockatiel that's startled or frightened may try to make itself as

difficult to see as possible by standing very erect with its crest held straight up. The bird will relax and resume a more normal posture when it feels the danger is past.

Beak Grinding

At times, you'll be sitting quietly and suddenly notice a faint, rumbly little noise coming from your cockatiel. Looking over, you might see that the bird's beak is moving slightly, and the sound is coming from the bird grinding its beak. This can happen when the bird is either in or out of the cage, and frequently occurs in the evenings just before bed. It's often accompanied by a slight puffing of the feathers and the bird may turn its head to rest on its back. It's a sign of a contented, happy, and possibly sleepy cockatiel. If you hear it when the bird is perched on your shoulder, it's a sign that your bird not only trusts you, but is happy to be with you.

Standing on One Foot

In general, a cockatiel standing on one foot isn't a sign of anything in particular, except that the bird wants to give its foot a rest. You would, too, if you stayed on your feet night and day. Many birds will stand on one foot to sleep. If your bird constantly keeps one foot tucked up,

A surprised cockatiel will stand very erect with its crest raised straight up.

however, you might want to have a veterinarian look at it, as this may indicate an injury or illness.

A Good Shake

A cockatiel will frequently shake its body vigorously, raising a large cloud of dust and dander. This is roughly the equivalent of when a person stretches. It feels good, stretches the muscles, and gets the blood flowing. Loose feathers may also be shaken loose, but this is not a problem.

Beak Tapping

When a cockatiel taps or wipes its beak on its perch, it's generally either trying to get your attention or is expressing its frustration over something. In the case of beak wiping, sometimes the obvious interpretation is the right one—the bird has something on its beak and is trying to get it off.

Yawning

There are possibly three different meanings behind a yawn, and the bird's other body language will help you interpret exactly what the bird is trying to tell you.

The first reason for a yawn is, obviously, because the bird is getting sleepy. The yawning may be accompanied by beak grinding, standing on one foot, and "hunkering down" with its feathers slightly puffed and its head nestled against its body or turned about so that the bird's "chin" rests on its back. When you see this

Birds yawn when they're tired, just like humans.

happening, it's time to leave the bird in its cage and let it take its nap.

Yawning can also be a sign of affection, a signal that your cockatiel would be willing to regurgitate for you if you wanted. When yawning means "I love you," the bird will also stand up straight and tall, bright-eyed and ready to interact.

Yawning can be a sign of aggression when the beak gapes open for a prolonged period, the head sways back and forth like a snake charmer, and the movement is accompanied by hissing or lunging. When you see this, the bird is clearly saying *back off*! Unless you're in a situation where it's important to move the bird for its own safety, it's best to just back away until it calms down.

Chapter Nine
Diet and Nutrition

The choices you make for your cockatiel's diet will do more than any other single thing you do to improve both the length and quality of its life. Although, traditionally, cockatiels have been fed diets of sunflower seed and millet, they are the nutritional equivalent of junk food, high in fat and low in nutrition. When cockatiels eat nothing but seeds, the birds are more likely to be overweight and to experience heart and liver damage. Scientists are still researching the nutritional needs of and best foods for pet birds, and although the ideal diet is still being perfected, there are several things to keep in mind when planning your bird's diet.

Comfort Foods

No matter what kind of diet you ultimately decide to feed your cockatiel, it's generally best to start it off in its new home with the same food it ate before it came to you. Familiar and favorite foods can be just as comforting to cockatiels as they are to people, and having their customary food available in their new home will make the transition that much less stressful. This means starting off with at least a few days' supply of the brand, flavor, and size of food that your cockatiel was eating at the seller's, if possible.

In addition, if you try to feed your cockatiel an unfamiliar food as soon as you bring it home, it's entirely possible that the cockatiel won't recognize the new food as something edible and will actually go hungry instead of eating it. There are several steps you can take to ease the transition from one food to another, including mixing the new food in the same dish as the old, changing the way the food is presented to the bird, and actually eating the food yourself in front of the bird as an example. During the first few days in its new home, however, familiar foods are the best.

Staple Foods

Seeds—No Longer a Staple

If you ask someone who kept a cockatiel as recently as ten or twenty years ago what her bird ate, chances are she'll tell you that she fed it a seed mix designed specifically for cockatiels. The recommended diet for many years, this was essentially a parakeet seed mix with sunflower seeds mixed in. Birds ate it, lived for maybe 12 or 15 years, then died. Now that more's known about avian nutritional requirements, a cockatiel's potential life span has grown to 15 to 20 years. Not only that, but the quality of life has improved—a bird that's healthy and well nourished will automatically feel better than a bird that's obese and malnourished.

Seed mixes can still be given, but they should not be your cockatiel's sole food. Feed them to your bird as you would eat sweets yourself, sparingly, as a special treat, but not as the mainstay of your bird's diet.

It's also worth noting that, although commercial seed mixes packaged for cockatiels are bad, birdseed intended for wild birds is even worse. Wild birdseed is usually designed for outdoor birds that are exposed to the elements, providing them with calories they need to maintain their body temperature in cold weather. In other words, the seeds in wild birdseed provide the very fats that are harmful to your cockatiel.

Anther problem with wild birdseed is the fact that it may not be as fresh as pet-quality seed. Pet birdseed is sold all year round, whereas wild birdseed is largely a seasonal product. Consequently, the wild birdseed that doesn't sell over the course of the winter may be kept until the cold weather returns, and thus it's more likely to be stale than the seed marketed for pets.

Grains and Cereals

Similar to seeds but with more nutritional value and less fat, grains and cereals can make up a significant portion of your cockatiel's diet. You can share the same grains and cereals that you eat with your cockatiel. Commercial cereals such as corn or wheat flakes, oat cereal, rice squares, or any other non-sugary breakfast cereal can be safely fed to your bird. Cooked foods such as brown rice, wheat bread, pasta, corn, cornbread, muffins, unsalted crackers, or croutons are all good sources of carbohydrates and are generally enjoyed by cockatiels. As with humans, foods made with "enriched flour" are not as beneficial as ones made with "whole grain" or "whole wheat," and foods made with no salt or that are low sodium are better than ones that are salted.

Pellets

Pelleted bird food is designed to be a complete nutritional package all in one processed food. Most companies that make pellets claim that all you ever need to give your bird to eat is pellets supplemented by water. There is no doubt that they contain more vitamins and minerals than seeds and can benefit a bird who's suffering from nutritional deficiencies. There are just two problems with pellets.

The first is that most birds don't seem to like them. A bird that's eaten them from the time it was a fledgling will continue to eat them with gusto, but a bird that's been raised on any

Combating Seed Moths

If you feed your cockatiel seeds, you may notice webs mixed in with the seeds and/or a sudden infestation of small white and brown moths. Seed moths, also known as "flour moths" and "pantry moths," are harmless insects that feed on seeds while in their larval stage. They won't harm your cockatiel, even if the bird eats them along with the seed—in fact, they're a source of protein.

If you'd prefer not to have moths fluttering around your home (and who wouldn't?), you can kill the larvae by keeping the seed in the freezer. Adult seed moths can be controlled using moth traps, which are available at most pet stores and pet supply sources. These traps work a lot like flypaper. A small square coated with moth pheromones is placed in the center of a piece of very sticky paper, which in turn is placed in a box to help keep you and your bird from getting stuck yourself. The pheromones are odorless to humans but will attract the moths into the trap. They fly in, get stuck, and die. When the traps get fully, simply throw them away. There are no pesticides involved, and so they are safe to keep in the same room as your cockatiel.

other diet will be extremely reluctant to change over to pellets and may go on a hunger strike rather than switch. There are several different techniques for converting the bird to this healthier diet, ranging from soaking them in fruit juice to mixing them with the current food and gradually changing the proportions so that there's more pellet and less of the other food until the dish contains nothing but pellets to cutting the bird off "cold turkey" from its favored food. Most packages of pellets offer different suggestions for how to change a bird into a pellet eater on the back of the bag.

The second problem with an all-pellet diet is that many cockatiel breeders have reported a link between this diet and cockatiel deaths due to visceral gout. As of this writing, there's no definitive proof of this correlation. Suspected causes include the artificial colors or perfumes used in pellets, or possibly the preservatives added to keep them fresh. Because of this, many people prefer to feed their cockatiels organic pellets that are free of artificial colors and preservatives. Others prefer to incorporate pellets as a part of their cockatiel's diet, but not feed them exclusively.

My own preference is to do a sort of balancing act. I feed my cockatiels a combination of cereals, fresh foods, and pellets, with seeds as the occasional treats. Because my cockatiels don't seem to like pellets, I toss a handful into the batter when I make them Birdie Bread (see recipe). It's the easiest way to get the birds to eat them; they get some of the nutritional benefits of pellets but less risk of developing gout.

Vegetables and Fruits

Fruits and vegetables are just as good for your cockatiel as they are for you. My experience is that cockatiels tend to prefer vegetables over fruit, but there are exceptions and both will usually be eaten gladly.

For the most part, the same rules that apply to humans when it comes to fruits and vegetables apply to birds as well. Foods contain the same vitamins and nutrients whether a human eats them or a bird does, so if a certain food is a good source of iron for you, it will be for your cockatiel as well. Similarly, foods that are lacking in nutritional value for you will be of minimal value to your bird. For example, foods like broccoli and spinach are good, while foods like iceberg lettuce are not as beneficial.

Fresh produce contains slightly more vitamins and minerals than vegetables that have been canned, cooked, or frozen. If you do use canned or frozen foods, those that contain no or low sodium are best. In deference to their small beaks, it's better to give cockatiels sliced fruits and vegetables. Even a small fruit like a grape can be a challenge for a

cockatiel to eat because of its round shape and relatively thick peel.

With the exception of avocados, which should *never* be fed to any pet bird, the fruits and vegetables that you enjoy are also safe for your bird to eat. It's perfectly fine for you to give your bird a tablespoon of whatever fruit or vegetable you're making for dinner. Cockatiels don't even mind if you feed them the leftovers off your plate when you finish your meal; in fact, feeding them leftovers is a healthy and convenient way to increase their nutritional intake.

The more variety you can provide in your tiel's diet, the healthier it is likely to be.

If you have a bird that is particularly reluctant to try new foods, there are several ways to encourage it to be more adventurous. One is to share what you're eating, making sure that the bird sees you making a big fuss over how good it is and how much you enjoy it before breaking off a piece and offering it to your bird. (Because you have bacteria in your mouth that's potentially harmful to your cockatiel, you don't want to give it the part you've actually bitten into.)

If seeing you enjoy the fresh food doesn't work, try varying the presentation a little. Offer chopped apples rather than sliced. Try shredded carrots rather than diced. Hang spinach from the roof of the cage rather than laying it in the bowl. Wedge a leaf of kale between the cage bars. Anything that makes the food seem more interesting may be enough to induce your cockatiel to try it.

Veggie Strategy

One great way to increase the variety of fresh foods that you feed your bird, and to save time and money while you're at it, is to buy your bird's vegetables at your local grocery's salad bar. The veggies are already washed, peeled, sliced, and shredded, and you can get a full day's allotment of vegetables—a leaf of spinach, some shreds of carrot, and maybe a ring of bell pepper—for just pennies.

Birdie Bread Recipe

Just as with children, a great way to get cockatiels to eat healthy foods they don't like is to hide them in another recipe. Birdie Bread is ideal for this. The recipe can be followed very loosely, and you can vary the types and amounts of vegetables and pellets depending on what you have on hand.

6 ounce box of corn muffin mix
6 ounce jar of baby food (dark
   green or yellow vegetables are
   best)
1 egg, with crushed shell
½ cup of pelleted bird food
½ cup of fruits or vegetables (leftovers work well)

Add baby food and egg (with shell) to the corn muffin mix. Stir well. Add vegetables. Mix well. Pour Into greased small loaf pan or greased muffin tins. Bake according to package directions for the size of pan you're using. Cool and serve to your bird. Be careful to warn other family members not to sample— they won't appreciate biting into the egg shells! Bread or muffins can be sliced into smaller portions and frozen, then taken out, thawed, and served daily.

One thing to watch out for when feeding fresh produce is spoilage. Sliced fruits or vegetables with their moist innards exposed to air become breeding grounds for potentially harmful bacteria. For this reason, it's best to place fruits and vegetables in a separate dish from other foods, and to remove them from the cockatiel's vicinity after an hour or two.

Mixing It Up

The perfect diet for a cockatiel is still a work in progress. Different "experts" will tell you different things. My own approach is to feed the widest variety of foods possible. This way, if one food is lacking in a certain nutrient, I figure the birds will get It when they eat another type of food.

I consider this approach to feeding birds perfect not only because it keeps my birds healthy, but because I think it adds to their quality of life. Even if pellets did turn out to be the perfect food nutritionally and came in a taste that all birds seemed to enjoy, I wouldn't want to deny my birds the pleasure and anticipation of having something new and tempting in their dish every day. Think about it: If consuming nothing but a nutritional formula would add two years to your life, wouldn't you still

want to indulge in the occasional steak, salad, or chocolate cake?

Heat and Eat Mixes

If you spend any time in the bird supply aisle of your local pet store, you may notice packages of "heat and eat" food mixes. Although the brand names and ingredients vary, these packages generally contain a mixture of grains, pastas, dehydrated fruits and vegetables, and occasionally even some spices. You add the mixture to boiling water and cook it until the grains and pasta are soft.

These mixes can make a wonderful addition to your cockatiel's diet, although it may take a bit of trial and error before you discover exactly which brand and flavor your bird

Foods High in Vitamin A

Vegetables:
Carrots
Sweet potatoes
Spinach
Collard greens
Winter squash
Peppers
Broccoli

Fruits:
Cantaloupe
Apricots
Papaya
Watermelon
Peaches
Nectarines

Non-Dairy Foods High in Calcium

Vegetables:
Bok choi
Beet greens
Dandelion greens
Kale
Mustard greens
Soybeans
Spinach
Swiss chard
Turnip greens

Fruits:
Blackberries
Currants
Mulberries
Oranges
Prickly pear
Prunes
Raisins
Raspberries
Rhubarb

For the more adventurous cook, it's also possible to use the packaged store mixes for inspiration to come up with your own heat and eat mix, combining the rice, pasta, grains, nuts, and vegetables that you have on hand to make a hot meal for your bird. Just as with the prepackaged varieties, you can cook a large amount and then freeze it into conveniently dispensed portions. Seeing your pet cockatiel enjoying a creation that you concocted just for it is a very rewarding experience, and cockatiels truly appreciate their food!

Treats

Another item that you may find in the bird food aisle are small packages of a specially formulated treat designed to be tasty and give the bird a bit of variety in its diet. These may be high in fat (particularly if they contain nuts) and relatively low in nutritional value, but given occasionally, they are fine for your bird.

Eggs and Dairy

Because birds don't give birth to live offspring and nurse their babies, cockatiels are not set up to digest the lactose in milk and should not be allowed to drink it. They are able to digest dairy products, such as cheese and yogurt, that contain lactase as opposed to lactose, and these can be good sources of calcium when given in small amounts.

Although it seems a little bit cannibalistic, cooked eggs are actually a good source of protein and are very beneficial for birds. They become an

favors. These mixes generally come with instructions for how to prepare small amounts in case you own a single bird, or you can cook the entire package at once, divide the finished product into ice cube trays, and pop one out to heat in the microwave when you're ready to feed it to your bird. These mixes can be made even healthier if you add your own vegetables to the pot while they're cooking. Be sure to let the mixture cool a little and stir it before offering it to the bird to eliminate hot spots that might burn its mouth.

An occasional treat, such as this millet spray, is fine, as long as it doesn't form the basis of the bird's diet.

even better source of nutrition when you crush the egg's shell and cook it up with the egg; the shells are an excellent source of calcium.

Foods to Avoid

As a general rule of thumb, what's bad for you is bad for your bird, and foods that contain caffeine, alcohol, fats, and salt should all be avoided. Don't let your bird sip your alcoholic drink or morning cup of coffee, don't feed it potato chips or French fries, and keep your chocolate to yourself. If your bird gets a taste of one of these forbidden foods, don't panic— a single taste isn't likely to be fatal. Do consider, however, the difference in size between you and your bird,

and how much more detrimental one of these forbidden foods would be to your cockatiel, with its 2½–3⅓ ounce (80–100 gram) body. The cumulative effects of any of these detrimental foods will be exponentially greater for your cockatiel, so keep your bird away from them.

Avocado Alert!

While cockatiels thrive on eating most fresh fruits and vegetables, there is one major exception: avocados. While avocados are harmless to humans, they are toxic to exotic birds such as cockatiels. *Never* feed your cockatiel avocados or foods that are made with avocado, such as guacamole.

Chapter Ten
Safety

In a lot of ways, having a cockatiel is like having a toddler. The difference is that in a couple of years, your toddler will become more self-sufficient and can be watched less closely, while you'll never be able to leave the cockatiel out of its cage unsupervised, no matter how old it gets. Add to that the fact that this "toddler" can fly, and you begin to get an idea of just how important it is to be extra vigilant when it comes to your cockatiel's safety.

Wing Trimming

Probably the single greatest thing you can do to keep your cockatiel safe is to trim its wings. A bird that can fly can get into many more dangerous situations than one that's "grounded." The exception to this is if you have small children who might try to grab the bird or other pets who might view the bird as prey. In these cases, your bird may be safer being able to take flight if a dangerous situation occurs. I have three cats, and during the winter months, when the cats spend most of their time in the house, I let all of the birds' wings grow out. In ten years of having both cats and birds, we've never had an incident, but since the cats move faster than I do, I feel it's safer to let the birds be able to fly if they feel threatened. I will sometimes clip a bird's wings if I'm going to be taking it out of the house, such as to a school or summer camp to talk about birds. In that case, I figure it's safer to make certain that the bird can't take off if it gets startled by fast-moving children in an unfamiliar place. Not only do I worry about the bird being able to fly out an open door and get lost, but it's also extremely possible that it might see what it thinks is an open flight path and end up crashing into a window by mistake.

Lost Birds

There are few things more heartbreaking than having a momentary lapse that allows your bird to fly out the door and get lost. Pet birds are not equipped to survive outdoors—they have no survival skills, no knowledge of how to find food, and won't be able to find their way home alone. A lost bird is vulnerable to cars, predators, starvation, and thirst. A few lucky birds may someday be returned to their owners, but the odds are against it.

Loss prevention is an important part of cockatiel ownership. Try to keep the bird's cage and play areas in rooms that don't have a door leading directly to the outside. Don't take the bird outside with you, even if the wings are clipped. Make sure the bird isn't behind you when you open the door for a guest, or to let a dog or cat in or out. Never answer the door with your bird on your shoulder. And never assume that because the bird's wings were clipped, that it won't be able to fly. If a stiff wind catches it just the wrong way, even a wing-clipped bird can achieve a controlled flight and gain altitude.

There are several other steps you can take to increase the likelihood of recovering your bird in case it ever gets lost, but you have to take them *before* the bird flies away.

First, if your bird has a leg band, write down the number and keep it in a safe place. The average person will not be able to trace you through the information on the leg band, but knowing the leg band number can help you make sure that any calls you get about found birds really are about your bird and not a scam for the reward money.

Second, make sure that you have a clear photograph of your bird that could be used in "Missing Bird" posters or a newspaper ad, particularly if your bird has unique markings. Digital photos are best because they can be used to make posters on your home computer. The best places to put posters are where large numbers of people will see them— bus stops, grocery stores, pet stores, animal shelters, veterinary offices, and near schools. Make sure that your poster has all of the pertinent information: when and where the bird went missing, how to reach you, the bird's name and any distinguishing characteristics, and whether or not a reward is offered.

Third, make an audio recording of your bird when it's playing happily or making a flock call. You can play the recording at full volume in your yard in hopes that your cockatiel will hear it and return to your yard.

Microchips: The latest technology for recovering lost pets is microchips—small computer chips that are implanted under the skin and can be read when an electronic scanner is waved over the animal's body. The scanner reveals a code number that is registered to the owner and kept on file with the microchip company. Once the microchip company is notified that a stray animal has been found with one of its chips implanted in it, the company notifies the owner with the news that the bird has been found. Most animal shelters and many veterinarians now have the scanners on site and will gladly scan any stray birds that are brought to them.

Microchips work very well in dogs and cats, but as tiny as they are, they may still be too large for an animal as small as a cockatiel. The general rule of thumb is not to microchip

any animal that weighs less than 3.5 ounces (100 g). An average, healthy cockatiel weighs between 2.8–3.5 ounces (80 and 100 g), and therefore many veterinarians and breeders do not recommend microchipping cockatiels. Because the 100-gram cutoff is just a rule of thumb and not a strict guideline, individual veterinarians may be willing to microchip a cockatiel, but most seem to feel that the size of the chip will bother a bird of that size. It is probable, however, that as the technology becomes more advanced, even smaller microchips will be developed. Ask your veterinarian about them if you are interested in having a microchip implanted in your bird.

Cockatiel Hazards

Toxic Metals

You've probably heard that ingesting certain metals, such as lead or mercury, leads to severe health consequences or even death in humans. The same danger exists for cockatiels—only, because of their small size, exposure to these toxic metals can lead to even more serious consequences.

Metal toxicity can be a little confusing because some metals, such as zinc, are not only safe in small quantities but necessary as trace minerals in both human and cockatiel diets. Taken in large quantities, however, zinc can lead to anemia and stunted growth and develop-

Three Unexpected Household Dangers
1. Avocado and foods containing avocado are poisonous to all types of parrots and other birds.
2. Cat saliva contains *Pasteurella*, a bacteria that is toxic to parrots.
3. Nonstick pans and other cookware containing PTFE emit toxic fumes at high temperatures.

ment. Fortunately, zinc poisoning is quite rare.

Other metals, such as lead, mercury, and caladium, are much more toxic and thus more likely to result in catastrophic consequences, even when ingested in very small quantities. Symptoms of heavy metal poisoning include loss of balance or coordination, paralysis, blindness, vomiting, diarrhea, unexplained weight loss, loss of appetite, bleeding from the mouth or nostrils, lethargy, and convulsions. Any of these symptoms should be viewed as potentially life threatening. Caught early, metal toxicity can be treated, but if it goes on long enough for neurological damage to occur, the consequences are irreversible and your cockatiel will never completely recover.

Beyond treatment, it's crucial that the source of the toxic metal be found in order to stop the bird from ingesting more of it. Items that frequently contain toxic metals include linoleum, the metal wrappers on

some wine bottles, very old paints—either on walls, old toys, or decorations—the connectors on stained glass, mercury-based thermometers, weights used to hold down draperies or for fishing, batteries, some wires, and the material used to solder metal pieces together.

If your bird is diagnosed as suffering from metal toxicity and you are unable to positively identify the source of exposure, then for the bird's future health and safety you should remove it to an entirely new environment—possibly to a new cage that you are certain contains no soldered pieces, and to a room containing all-new items. Hopefully, by doing so, you'll eliminate the bird's exposure to the source of the toxic metal.

Poisonous Plants

Live, lush plants are an asset to any household, but not all houseplants are safe to keep with cockatiels in the house. Because cockatiels are curious birds and like to explore things by tasting them, any plant in the house is likely to be subjected to nibbling at some point. Even some cut flowers and greenery can pose a threat.

The safest thing to do is to make sure that the plants you keep indoors are nontoxic to cockatiels. Some of the more commonly kept houseplants are listed here according to whether or not they pose a threat to cockatiels. If you do want to keep a plant that's toxic, there are steps you can take to prevent the cockatiel from getting into it, such as keeping it in a closed-off room, growing it in a covered glass terrarium, or—ironically enough—keeping it in a closed birdcage. In my house, I have a snippet of English ivy that came from my great-grandparents'

Houseplant Safety—Poisonous Plants

Amaryllis bulbs
Avocado (fruit and plant)
Azalea leaves
Caladium leaves
Castor beans
Clematis
Daffodil bulbs
Delphinium
Dieffenbachia leaves (also known as "dumb cane")
Eggplant plant (fruit is okay)
Elephant ear leaves and stems
English ivy
Foxglove (leaves and seeds)
Hemlock
Holly berries
Horse chestnut twigs and nuts
Hyacinth bulbs
Jack-in-the-Pulpit
Juniper stems, needles, and berries
Larkspur
Laurel
Lily of the valley
Lobelia
Locoweed
Lords and ladies
Marijuana leaves
Mistletoe
Monkshood
Morning glories
Narcissus bulbs
Nightshade
Philodendron leaves and stems
Poinsettia
Poison oak and ivy
Pokeweed (also known as "inkberry")
Privet
Rhododendron
Rhubarb leaves
Snowdrop
Sweet pea fruit
Tobacco leaves
Virginia creeper
Wisteria
Yew

house; to keep the birds away from it, the ivy is in an antique-looking birdcage, an arrangement that provides both sentiment and safety. Realistic-looking artificial plants and flowers can also be safely used in place of the real thing.

When you get a cockatiel, you need to make sure both new and existing houseplants are safe for your bird.

Houseplant Safety—Safe Plants

African violets
Bachelor's buttons
Bamboo
Boston fern
Bottlebrush
Camellia
Canna lily
Canterbury bells
Chicken and hens
Cockscomb
Coral bells
Cornflower
Crape myrtle (also spelled "crepe myrtle")
Creeping Charlie
Dwarf palm
Feather fern
Fireweed
Gloxinia
Grape hyacinth
Grape ivy
Hollyhocks
Nerve plant
Night-blooming cereus
Old man cactus
Peperomia
Persian violet
Piggyback plant
Ponytail
Prayer plant
Purple baby tears
Purple passion vine
Rabbit's foot fern
Spider plant
Swedish ivy
Sweet William
Tulip tree
Umbrella plant
Venus flytrap
Wax plant
Zebra plant

If you have questions about a particular type of plant, the ASPCA has a more comprehensive list of nontoxic plants on its Web site and will answer questions about specific plants that are not listed by e-mail at napcc@aspca.org. However, the ASPCA cautions that its e-mail isn't monitored 24/7, so if your cockatiel has ingested a plant that you are not certain of, don't wait for an e-mail response: contact your veterinarian immediately. If your cockatiel has eaten a suspect plant and you can't reach your veterinarian, you can call the Animal Poison Control Center at (888) 426-4435, which is open 24 hours a day, 365 days a year, but be aware that there is a charge for its assistance.

If you do find yourself in a situation where your cockatiel has sampled one of your houseplants, bring both the leaf that it has nibbled on as well as either the plant or an uneaten sample of the leaves. This will help the veterinarian figure out how much of the toxic material the bird has ingested as well as to determine exactly what kind of plant is involved. Many plants are known by more than one name, and seeing

536°F (232°C), it begins to deteriorate and gives off a toxic gas that is lethal to parrots and other exotic birds, damaging the lungs and causing death within a very short period of time. It may also result in flu-like symptoms in humans who breathe in the heated fumes.

Although most people cook at much lower temperatures than that at which PTFE begins to deteriorate, an unattended pan forgotten on the stovetop may well reach the danger point. It's best to keep your cockatiel out of the kitchen, especially when you're cooking. This eliminates not only the danger of its breathing in toxic gases but also the chance of it landing on the stove and being burned. You can switch to cast iron or stainless steel pans.

Self-cleaning ovens are frequently coated with PTFE and work at high temperatures. Because of the toxic fumes given off by this chemical and aerosol oven cleaners, it's best to avoid cleaning the oven with the bird in the house. If this is unavoidable, the bird should be removed to the farthest possible end of the house with the windows open while cleaning is underway.

PTFE is also used in many other household products, such as hair dryers, electric curling and straightening irons, space heaters, and indoor electric grills. If you have any

a sample of the plant may help the veterinarian determine the best course of treatment.

Nonstick Cookware

Most indoor threats to cockatiels are obvious if you just use a little common sense. However, one of the most dangerous things in your house is actually a hidden threat—a chemical called polytetrafluoroethylene, or PTFE for short. PTFE is commonly used in nonstick cookware, such as Teflon or Silver Stone. When PTFE reaches a temperature of

of these products that contain PTFE, try to avoid using them in the presence of your cockatiel. It's much better to be safe than sorry.

Water Danger

Cockatiels may enjoy bathing in a shallow bowl or pan full of water, or being sprayed by a plant mister, but the fact of the matter is that they can't swim. Consequently, the cockatiel owner must be vigilant to ensure that the bird never gets into deep water and drowns.

Water hazards can include indoor ponds or water fountains, fish tanks, sinks full of water, bathtubs, pans full of liquid, open toilet bowls, and even glasses of your favorite beverage. Never leave a cockatiel unsupervised near any open source of water or other liquid. It could slip, fall in, and not be able to extricate itself.

Also, cockatiels should never be allowed to ingest alcoholic beverages. Being both curious and social, a cockatiel may well try to sample whatever glass it sees people drinking from. But remember: Your body is several thousand times the size of your bird's, and even a small amount of alcohol can have a devastating effect on the bird's body.

Electrical Wires

Cockatiels are curious creatures who like to explore things with their mouths. This makes electrical wires particularly dangerous objects, because of the risk of electric shock. Keep all electrical wiring out of reach of the cockatiel. Extra-long cords

can be bundled and fastened up off the floor, where curious beaks cannot get at them. Some people also use pipes or PVC tubes to run their electrical cords through so that the enclosed cords are essentially out of harm's way.

Chemicals and Cleaners

Cleaners and other chemical substances pose a danger to your cockatiel, not just because they can be ingested but because of the fumes they give off. To keep your bird safe, move it to the other end of the house whenever you use strong chemicals or cleaners, such as oven cleaner, bleach, or drain cleaner. The bird should never be present when you

have these chemicals out, and you should wait until their accumulated fumes have had a chance to dissipate before bringing it back. If you can still smell them, keep the bird away.

Many people opt to use organic or homemade cleaners, which contain less-dangerous ingredients, to decrease the risk of exposure to toxic chemicals for their cockatiels.

How to Medicate Your Cockatiel

Because taking a sick pet cockatiel to the veterinarian is always a somewhat stressful situation, you may not be able to think of all the questions that you should ask, or to recall afterward everything that your veterinarian has told you to do. Here, then, is a step-by-step guide for how to administer medication to your cockatiel.

Powdered medications: Frequently vitamins or another dietary supplement, powdered medications can be sprinkled on a very small amount of "heat and eat"-style bird food, either one that you make yourself or one that you buy from the pet store. If you mix the powder into your bird's drinking water, you can't be certain how much the bird will ingest, and foreign substances introduced into the water can encourage the growth of potentially harmful bacteria. If you simply try sprinkling the powder over the bird's dry food, it will fall uneaten between the seeds and collect with the chaff at the bottom of the dish.

If you don't have any heat and eat mix on hand and don't have the ingredients to make your own, try any sort of moist "people food" such as spaghetti or mashed vegetables. Give the bird just a small amount with the powder sprinkled on it. Don't give the bird too much of this food at once; you can give "seconds" as a reward once it's eaten the portion with the powder mixed in.

Liquid medications: Most veterinarians will supply you with plastic syringes if you need to give your bird a liquid medication. If he or she forgets, or if you misplace them, you can improvise by dipping a plastic spoon into boiling water and then squeezing the sides of the bowl to form a funnel, or by using a plastic eyedropper or a medicine dispenser intended for human infants. Many pet supply dealers carry syringes as well.

Simply adding the medicine to the bird's water source is not a good idea unless you are specifically

First Aid Kit

The best time to think about first aid is before you actually need to apply it. Because you can't predict what kind of emergency you may someday face, here is a list of items to have on hand just in case.

- Hospital cage (See page 122; this cage also makes an excellent place to store the items in your first aid kit.)
- Heating pad
- Syringe(s)
- Tweezers
- Gauze bandages
- Surgical tape
- Cotton balls
- Electrolyte solution (such as Pedialyte)
- Hand-feeding formula (so that you can feed your bird using a syringe in case of beak injury)
- Styptic powder or stick (If you don't have it on hand, corn starch or flour can be used.)
- Small scissors
- Pepto-Bismol or other aid for indigestion (A small, travel-sized bottle will do.)
- Latex gloves
- Hydrogen peroxide
- Hand-sanitizing lotion
- Small bottle of antiseptic spray
- Chemically activated ice pack and hand warmers
- Phone numbers for your veterinarian and the animal poison control center
- Your first aid kit is also a good place to store this book, with the pages on first aid bookmarked.

instructed to do so. You can't control how much of the medication the bird actually takes in, and your cockatiel may be disinclined to drink any if the medication alters the taste of the water.

It's a little tricky to get a liquid medicine into an unwilling cockatiel, and you have to be careful about which direction you squirt the medicine into the bird. If you come at it from the wrong side, you risk getting the liquid into the bird's air pipe, which is harmful. It's much easier to administer the medication if you measure it out into the syringe or dropper first, *before* you get the bird. Hold the bird directly in front of you, facing you. Wrapping the bird in a hand towel first with only its head sticking out generally makes the process much simpler. You can keep the bird still by holding the palm and last three fingers of your left hand over its back so that it can't open its wings, while placing your thumb and forefinger on either side of the head to keep it still.

Hold the syringe or dropper in your right hand. You want to put the tip into the mouth from your right side, so that it squirts to your left. (If

Evacuation Pack

In addition to a first aid kit, it's also a good idea to have the supplies for an evacuation pack in your cockatiel's hospital cage. That way, you'll have everything you need ready to go on a moment's notice should a natural disaster threaten. The hospital cage itself can become a suitable evacuation cage in the event that you need to fit as many of your possessions into your car as possible. Supplies for an evacuation pack should include several bottles of water and a half gallon to gallon-sized bag of your bird's food, both of which you should rotate, replacing them with fresh every few months. In addition, include a piece of paper with your name, the bird's name, your address, cell phone number, and e-mail address in the event that you and your bird become separated, as well as contact information for a friend or relative not traveling with you in case that something happens to you. Any medications your bird is taking should be taken with you and listed on this paper, along with a photograph of the bird and its leg band number, if there is one, so that you can prove it is your bird in the event that it flies off and is recovered by an animal rescue group.

you're holding the syringe in your right hand, it should be pretty obvious which direction you will be squirting from, because squirting from the left side while holding the syringe in your right hand will feel awkward and wrong.) Jimmy the beak open with the tip of the syringe or dropper and squirt the liquid in. Try to hold the head still until all of the medicine is in. The bird's inclination will be to twist its head at having its mouth invaded by a foreign substance, flinging the medication all over you and the surrounding area.

I generally try to give my bird a treat immediately after medicating it both by way of apology for the undignified handling and to help wash the taste out of its mouth. I usually slip on a pair of gardening gloves when I have to medicate any of my birds. Not only does it offer a slight layer of protection (although any bite through the glove is still going to hurt), but I want the bird to associate the unpleasantness with the gloves rather than with my hand.

There may also be times when an owner is instructed to give a bird medication by injection. In this case, it's best to have the veterinarian show you exactly how and where to administer it. Do not leave the veterinarian's office until you are certain that you are able to do this. If you are not comfortable with the idea, ask if your bird can be admitted so that trained staff can take over this task instead.

Chapter Eleven
Health

L ike all birds, cockatiels try to hide all signs of illness until they are too sick to conceal it any longer. Because of this, it's crucial that you take your bird to the veterinarian at the first sign that something might be wrong. The medical conditions mentioned in this chapter can only be diagnosed and treated by a veterinarian and are discussed to give you a starting place if your cockatiel is diagnosed with one of them. Do not attempt to diagnose or treat your bird based on what you read here.

Is Your Cockatiel Ill?

Weighing Your Bird
Because birds generally hide all symptoms of illness, it's frequently impossible for the owner to tell when a bird is sick. But there is one symptom that your cockatiel can't hide—weight loss. A sick cockatiel may experience a sudden, drastic drop in weight or a slow, gradual decrease that can't be explained by a change in the bird's diet.

It's possible to visually recognize that a cockatiel is too thin. If you can see or feel the keel bone—the long, narrow bone that runs vertically down the center of the chest—your bird is too thin. However, problems can be spotted earlier, and thus treated sooner, if you make it a practice to weigh your bird at regular intervals and keep track of fluctuations in its weight.

You can use either a dieter's scale or a postal scale, both of which register small amounts. Because the metric system is more precise than the English system, changes will be easier to recognize if you weigh your bird in grams rather than in ounces. (One ounce is equal to 28 grams, so there would be 28 different increments of change in grams before you would see a single unit of change in ounces.) Although there are special bird scales available that come equipped with a perch, I use a regular postal scale and simply have the bird stand on the weighing platform, and it works quite well.

Remember that small fluctuations in weight—those of just a few grams a day—are normal, just as a change of a few ounces would be normal for

It's very difficult to visually tell if a cockatiel is losing weight until the weight loss is quite drastic.

break down and digest their foods. Other, less helpful types of bacteria are also present, but these are not a problem unless they begin to flourish to the point where they outnumber and interfere with the useful types of bacteria.

A Gram stain is a test that determines the amounts of both "good" and "bad" bacteria in the bird's body by using samples taken from inside the bird's mouth and throat, around its vent area, or from its droppings. The helpful bacteria are called "Gram positive" while the harmful ones are called "Gram negative."

If the amount of Gram-negative bacteria is too high, the veterinarian may prescribe either a course of antibiotics or adding organic cider vinegar to the drinking water (on the theory that the increased acidity will reduce the levels of bacteria in the bird's digestive tract). The cider vinegar is followed by a product high in Gram-positive bacteria, designed to crowd out the number of Gram-negative bacteria.

Some veterinarians, however, do not advocate using Gram stain testing because they find it's not very helpful. Although it gives a quick and inexpensive look at the bacteria levels in the bird, it is not as accurate as a more expensive culture, does not directly test the site of many infections, and does not reveal all types of bacteria or viruses. Also, the mere presence of Gram-negative bacteria may not be indicative of illness—the bacteria could just be "passing through."

you, depending on the time of day or whether or not you've recently eaten. So don't panic if you notice that your bird is a couple of grams lighter one morning. Simply write the numbers down and keep track. A steady loss of weight for a week or longer indicates that it's time to call the veterinarian.

Gram Stain

Like people, birds normally have a large variety of bacteria living in their digestive systems. Most of the time, this bacteria is harmless. In fact, many types of bacteria help birds

Common Cockatiel Ailments

Aspergillosis

Aspergillus is a kind of fungus commonly found in soil, on some plants, and in decaying plant material. Its spores are very prevalent, and most of us breathe in small amounts of them every day with no perceptible effects. It poses a problem, however, when inhaled in large amounts or by someone with a compromised immune system. The resulting condition is called aspergillosis.

Aspergillosis in cockatiels is a very serious condition. The fungus takes hold in the bird's air sacs, making it difficult for the bird to breathe. It often appears in birds with insufficient immune systems or a vitamin A deficiency. It's somewhat less common today than it was when wild-caught birds were imported and kept in close quarters with large numbers of other birds in unsanitary conditions, but it can affect birds if they are exposed to it. It's treatable in the early stages, but the longer it's allowed to develop without treatment, the more difficult it is to cure. Left unchecked, this condition may be fatal.

Giardiasis

Giardia is a type of protozoan that is frequently found in dirty water or in the droppings of infected birds. It's particularly prevalent in birds who either drink water that has been defecated in or who eat droppings off the bottom of the cage. People can also be infected by giardiasis, frequently ingesting it while swimming in outdoor ponds, but there have been no reported cases of anyone contracting it from a cockatiel.

Cockatiels who are infected with giardiasis may look fairly healthy, or they may be very agitated and seem to be constantly itching, scratching, or even pulling their feathers out, particularly along the legs, flank, and on their back between the wings. Unexplained weight loss is also frequently seen. This condition is often diagnosed by microscopically examining a sample of the feces, and it is treated by antibiotic or antifungal medication, possibly supplemented by vitamins to help alleviate the malnutrition that the giardia causes and an antihistamine to relieve the itching.

Pacheco's Disease

The virus that causes Pacheco's disease is a strain of herpes virus, and so the alternate name for this disease is the psittacine herpes virus. Symptoms of this condition include lethargy, ruffled feathers, loss of appetite, sinusitis, diarrhea, and a change in the color of the droppings due to liver damage. Frequently, the first obvious sign of Pacheco's disease is that birds suddenly start to die several days after a new bird has been introduced. Pacheco's disease is particularly devastating because it is highly contagious and usually fatal. Birds that do manage to survive often become carriers of the virus and spread it to all other birds they come in contact with.

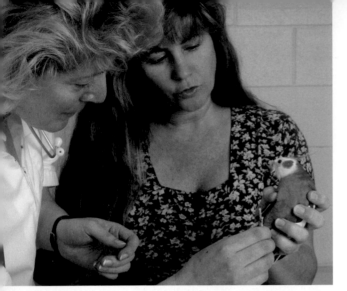

Because birds naturally try to hide signs of illness, annual checkups should be given even if the bird seems healthy.

Because Pacheco's disease is so highly contagious, any bird that is diagnosed with it should be immediately isolated from all other birds in the house. The infected bird's environment, including cage, dishes, perches, toys, and anything else the bird had contact with, should be thoroughly disinfected with a mixture of one part bleach to nine parts water.

A vaccine for Pacheco's disease is available, but because it may cause an adverse reaction, it is generally only given after a bird has been exposed to the virus, or to a bird that is known to carry the virus.

If you suspect your bird is sick, don't try to diagnose and treat the problem yourself—the delay in seeing a vet could well mean the difference between life and death!

Antiviral medications are currently being tried in birds that have been exposed to Pacheco's disease to help control the outbreak of Pacheco's within the flock and limit the number of deaths.

Polyoma

Polyoma is a disease caused by a virus that affects younger birds more seriously than older ones. It's one of the few conditions for which there is an effective vaccine, although the vaccine is ineffective once the bird has contracted the disease. Some birds that appear fairly healthy may be carriers; they may even test negative for polyoma if they are tested at a time when they are not actively shedding the virus. Consult with your avian veterinarian to decide whether or not your bird should be inoculated or tested for the disease.

Polyoma is always fatal in baby birds, but adults that contract it may survive if treated with a combination of antibiotics or antifungals, blood transfusions, and good, supportive care. Adults that are found to be carriers can live relatively normal, healthy lives, but they should be kept isolated from all non-infected/non-carrier birds. If you own a cockatiel that is a polyoma carrier and are able to keep it out of contact with other birds, there is no need to euthanize your pet. However, you should take care to practice exceptionally good hygiene when going to a location where there are uninfected birds, washing yourself thoroughly and changing your shoes and clothing.

When It's Time to See a Veterinarian

It's a good idea to contact your avian veterinarian if you see any of the following:

- A significant decrease in activity/energy
- Unkempt-looking feathers
- Feathers that are puffed in moderate temperatures
- Sleeping with both feet on the perch
- Huddling on the cage bottom with feathers puffed
- Discharge from eyes, nose, or anywhere on the body that should be dry
- Wheezing or audible breathing
- Tail pumping up and down to assist breathing
- Changes in color, quantity, or consistency of droppings that are not related to changes in diet (Note: Birds that are nesting or preparing to lay eggs normally have huge droppings.)
- A foul odor coming from either the bird or its droppings
- Drastic changes in weight
- Vomiting
- Seizures
- An accumulation of droppings that sticks to the feathers around the vent area
- Any sign of bleeding
- Wings or legs held at unnatural angles
- Growths, sores, or any other skin abnormality
- Crying or shying away when you try to get it to step up (if it's ordinarily tame)
- Impaired balance
- When you have a feeling that something isn't right with your bird, even if you can't put your finger on just what it is, trust your instincts!

The condition is spread when the virus is shed in the bird's droppings, or when the droppings dry and the dust from them becomes airborne, such as when you jostle them while cleaning the cage. It can also be transmitted by an infected parent to its chick, or through contact with an infected area, such as a dirty cage or nest box.

As mentioned polyoma is one of the few bird diseases that can be vaccinated against, although vacci-nation may not be necessary if you begin with a healthy bird, are not planning to put it in contact with other birds, and do not intend to breed. Again your avian veterinarian can best advise you.

Proventricular Dilation Disease

Proventricular dilation disease (or PDD) is a somewhat mysterious condition where the bird may either steadily lose weight in spite of eating

The preen gland, located under the feathers at the base of the tail, secretes an oil that helps keep the feathers healthy.

large amounts of food, or stop eating altogether, vomit, and pass undigested food in its droppings, leading to extreme weight loss. Because of this, it's sometimes referred to as "the wasting disease." Although some scientists think that it may be the result of a virus, the exact cause is unknown. The most recent treatments involve the use of steroids, but there is no known cure and PDD is usually fatal.

Psittacosis

Psittacosis, which is also known as chlamydiosis or "parrot fever," is noteworthy because it's one of the few diseases that can be transmitted from birds to humans. Birds infected with this disease may appear to be completely symptom-free. The dis-

ease can be latent for long periods of time, or the bird may simply be a carrier, which is one reason why a "new bird" visit to an avian veterinarian is so important. (However, at this point, there is no test for psittacosis that is 100 percent accurate.) When symptoms do present themselves, they are typical of a sick bird, including unexplained weight loss, nasal discharge and/or sneezing, watery eyes, lime-green droppings, and loss of appetite. Symptoms in humans may include a high fever, fatigue, and an atypical form of pneumonia. Although the disease is treatable, because it is transmittable to humans, veterinarians are required to report cases of it to government-run health organizations so that it can be tracked.

Psittacosis spreads when the bacteria that causes the disease is shed by the bird, either when it sneezes out infected nasal discharge, or through its droppings. The droppings of an infected bird dry, the resulting dust becomes airborne when disturbed (such as when the cage is cleaned), and this dust is breathed in by another bird or by a person, infecting them.

Emergency First Aid for Cockatiels

The following steps are intended only as a stopgap in the event that you can't get your cockatiel to a vet's in a timely manner. They are not intended as curative treatments, but they may be enough to prevent further damage or even death.

Bleeding

Cleanse the area gently with hydrogen peroxide or an over-the-counter antiseptic. Styptic powder or a styptic stick can be used if you have them, or you can sprinkle the wound with flour or baking soda to encourage clotting. If possible, cover the wound with a square of gauze and apply direct pressure. If the cuts are on the body, cover them with gauze and use an appropriately sized sock with holes cut out for the head and legs to keep the gauze in place until the bird can be seen by a veterinarian.

Broken Blood Feather

Some feathers, when they first break through the skin, contain blood vessels that are connected to the bird's circulatory system. These are referred to as "blood feathers" and if you look, you can actually see that the quill closest to the body has a dark purplish color because of the blood vessels inside. As the feather grows and matures, the blood vessels that go into the feather gradually close off and blood no longer flows into the quill, giving the quill a dull, gray color. This is why, when the feather molts naturally, you don't see any blood.

Blood feathers can be broken in flying accidents, when the bird thrashes during night frights, and through rough handling. There will be no doubt in your mind when this happens; the broken quill will begin to bleed. Sometimes the feather will stop bleeding on its own. If it doesn't, you need to take steps to stop the bleeding yourself.

Some people prefer to staunch the blood by applying a styptic stick to the broken end of the quill. While this may work, stopping the flow of blood this way can leave the feather vulnerable to further breaks. The feather could start to bleed again when the bird preens or if the broken feather is bumped. For this reason, the best course of action is to pull out the bleeding feather. Once the quill is out of the skin, the follicle will close and the bleeding will stop.

The easiest way to pull out an actively bleeding blood feather is to have two people—one to hold the bird and the other to extend the wing and actually pull the feather. The bird is likely to be upset, so it's best to loosely wrap the cockatiel's body in a towel, leaving the injured wing exposed. The cockatiel will feel a stinging sensation when the feather is pulled, the same way you might feel a sting when someone pulls a hair, so covering the bird will keep you from being bitten.

Once you have the bird restrained, gently extend the injured wing, pulling it out to the side the way it would naturally unfold. Grasp the broken quill firmly and literally pull it out of the skin. Make sure to pull the feather straight out, in the same direction in which the feather grew—don't twist the feather as you remove it. You can use your thumb and index fingers to grasp the broken quill and pull it out. Tweezers can be tried, but in my

Hospital Cages

If your bird is sick or injured, you may want to place it in a special "hospital cage" for its convalescence. A hospital cage is a smaller, more portable cage where your cockatiel can be isolated from other birds and kept quietly and without excitement while it recovers. A hospital cage is generally solid-sided to keep drafts from reaching your bird, and provides a way of regulating the temperature inside so that the bird can spend its energy on recovering rather than on maintaining its body temperature.

It's best to have a hospital cage prepared in advance, before you're faced with a medical emergency and need to scramble to find all of the components in a hurry. I keep the items that make up my cockatiel first aid kit in my hospital cage and store the whole thing in a closet off of my bird room, so that everything is convenient and easy to find when the need for it arises.

The easiest way to make an inexpensive hospital cage is to start with a box, fish tank, or small plastic cage with a ventilated cover. In my house, we use a plastic cage marketed for reptiles but that is light enough and large enough to serve our purpose. The cage should be big enough for the bird to stand up and turn around comfortably, approximately 9 inches by 12 inches (approximately 23 cm by 30 cm). It

may come with a cover. (If you're using a fish tank, you can buy a separate fitted screen cover or improvise one if you're using a cardboard box). Whatever you use for a cover, make sure that it has holes or slits to allow for proper ventilation.

Line the bottom of the hospital cage with a folded cloth. Towels or washcloths made of terry cloth are not suitable because your bird's toenails may get caught in the small loops of the material. Placing a folded paper towel on top of the cloth will make it easier both to clean the cage and to observe the bird's droppings. Small dishes for food and water can be placed on the cage floor so that your bird can eat or drink if it feels up to it.

Place a non-mercury-based thermometer inside the cage so that you can monitor the temperature inside. These types of thermometers may be available in pet supply stores. If you only have a mercury-based thermometer, you can use it at intervals, but don't leave it in the cage with the bird unsupervised, since the mercury is poisonous if the bird should decide to chew on the thermometer.

Place half of the hospital cage on top of a heating pad, setting the temperature so that it's between 85 and 90°F (29–32°C). By placing only half of the cage on top of the heating pad, you create warmer and cooler sections of the cage so the bird can move to wherever it is most comfortable. Use the thermometer to make sure that the temperature in the cage reflects the setting on the heating pad. Providing warmth will let your bird use the energy it would normally spend maintaining its body temperature to ward off shock or to fight off its illness instead.

Cover the top and all but one side of the cage with a towel to keep it dark and encourage the bird to rest. You can transport the bird in its hospital cage to the veterinarian as needed.

After the situation has been resolved, throw out the paper towel and wash the cloth you used to line the cage and the cover of the heating pad in hot water. Run the dishes through the dishwasher and wipe off the inside and outside of the hospital cage and the thermometer with a mixture of nine parts water to one part bleach. You can then store your avian first aid and evacuation kits inside the empty hospital cage and put the whole thing away until the next time it's needed.

A hospital cage helps to keep the patient warm, isolated, and easy to transport to the veterinarian. This bird was treated for psittacosis.

get a firm enough grasp to pull it out, take the bird to a veterinarian as soon as possible.

Burns

Flush with cold water to stop the burning and start to relieve the pain. If blisters are present or the wound is open, get the bird to the veterinarian as soon as possible to reduce the chances of a life-threatening infection.

Cat Bites

Flush with hydrogen peroxide and apply an antibiotic ointment. Pasteurella, a kind of bacteria found in cat's saliva, can cause death within 24 hours, so get the bird to a veterinarian ASAP.

Convulsions

Move the cockatiel to a box with solid walls (a cardboard box or hospital cage will do) and place a thick layer of folded cloth on the bottom to prevent the bird from hurting itself or catching its wings between the bars if it starts to thrash again.

Dehydration

This condition may occur if the bird has been away from its water supply for a period of time (such as if it was lost outside the home and recovered days later) or if it's experiencing vomiting or diarrhea. Instead of giving it plain water, offer the bird an electrolyte solution such as Pedialyte to restore it to health. Electrolyte solution, which is generally found in the baby food aisle of the grocery store, can also be used to mix baby formula in the event that you have to hand-

experience, they usually slip off the quill and the small size of the tweezers makes it hard to see what you are doing. The easiest way is to use a pair of needle-nosed pliers to grasp the broken quill as close to the skin as possible and pull it straight out with one steady yank. The bird might squawk when the quill is pulled out, but that's normal—it's not a pleasant feeling. The skin around the follicle should close up once the quill is gone, stopping the bleeding. Eventually a new feather will emerge to replace the one that's missing.

If you have a situation where multiple feathers are involved, pull the broken ones out one at a time. If you are too squeamish to pull out the bleeding blood feather, or if you can't

feed. Leftover electrolyte solution can be poured into ice cube trays and frozen, then stored in ziplock bags in the freezer for future use.

Diarrhea

If diarrhea is the result of something the bird ate, remove all fruits and vegetables from its cage and see if you can get the bird to eat boiled white rice or peanut butter. If your bird has not been eating foods that are likely to have made its bowels loose, bring it to the veterinarian as soon as possible to avoid dehydration and to check for a gastrointestinal infection. Both of these causes can be fatal if left untreated.

Egg Binding

(See page 130.)

Eye Problems

If something gets into the bird's eye and causes irritation, try to flush it out by squirting water over the affected eye using a syringe. Or, gently flush the eye out with cool water while holding the bird under the faucet.

Heatstroke

Spray or mist the bird with cool water. Encourage it to stand in a pie plate full of cool water, and keep the bird in a cool place until it recovers.

Poisoning

If the poison is non-corrosive, try to slow down the absorption of the poison by giving the cockatiel olive oil, raw egg whites, or Pepto-Bismol.

If your are not sure if what the bird has eaten is poisonous, or if a veterinarian is not available, call the Animal Poison Control Center at (888) 426-4435. There is a charge for calling, but they are available 24 hours a day, 7 days a week, 365 days a year. If there is going to be a delay in getting treatment, this call can be the difference between life and death.

Shock

Signs of shock in a bird include rapid, shallow breathing, puffed feathers, stillness, and/or sitting with the head turned and the eyes partially closed. Treat by moving the bird to a quiet, dimly lit place, and keeping it warm (between 86 and 90°F (30–32.2°C) is ideal) until you can get it to the veterinarian.

Vomiting

Vomiting is not the same as regurgitating, which is when your bird tries to feed you, its chick, or another bird as a sign of affection. A regurgitating bird may only open its mouth and bob its head. A bird that is vomiting may appear to be in distress and will not be able to stop vomiting if you say its name or otherwise distract it, whereas a bird that is regurgitating is in control of its actions and should be able to stop if you focus its attention on something else. A bird that is truly vomiting should be seen by a veterinarian as soon as possible, since vomiting can be a sign of an infection, an impacted crop, or poisoning, all of which are potentially fatal.

Chapter Twelve
Egg, Chick, Cockatiel

When it comes to egg laying, cockatiels are like the chickens of the parrot world. You may have a hen who lays eggs with alarming regularity, whether or not she is given a male or a nest box. Even if you don't intend to breed cockatiels, there are certain things you should know about cockatiel reproduction, particularly if you own a hen. This chapter will tell you what to look for, what to do, and when to intervene in the event that you suddenly find yourself staring at a small, white egg on the cage floor.

To Breed or Not to Breed?

Breeding cockatiels is not something that should be entered into lightly. If you are considering letting your cockatiels reproduce, there are several things that you need to take into account first.

Assuming that you wanted a pet cockatiel for a companion, you should be aware that even the tamest of cockatiels will undergo a significant personality change once it starts sitting on its eggs. You will no longer be the adored owner, its chief companion and beloved head-scratcher; instead you will be viewed as a potential threat to the eggs, someone to be driven off and even bitten if you get too close to them. The bird will return to its usual, friendly self once the ordeal is over. In fact, cockatiels are less ferocious about defending their chicks than they are their eggs.

Egg laying and the raising of chicks puts a physical strain on the parents as well. Much of the mother's nutritional reserve goes into the formation of the eggs, and just as some women need cesarian sections when they are unable to deliver their babies vaginally, some hens may be unable to successfully pass their eggs, a condition called egg binding, which can be fatal if left untreated.

If chicks hatch, the parents inevitably get less sleep and nutrition as they struggle to take care of not only themselves but a number of demanding young. The youngest chicks often do not survive because they can't compete with their bigger nest mates for the limited amount of food that the parents can supply.

If your birds reproduce, you need to be able to provide homes for all of the babies. One of the keys to cockatiels' survival in the wild is to breed often and have large clutches. A typical cockatiel pair may lay two to nine eggs (although five is typical) up to four times a year. Unless you can line up potential homes for all of these chicks, you may well find yourself with more cockatiels than you really want.

Raising chicks can be a delicate proposition as well. As mentioned, it's not unusual for the last one hatched to starve to death because it can't compete for food. If you opt to try to save it by hand-feeding, be aware that you'll be tied to that chick every two hours morning and night for the first week or so. Hand feeding is not a simple task, and a large number of things can go wrong—all resulting in the death of the chick you've tried so hard to save.

You should not decide to let your birds breed because you think selling the chicks will be a fast way to make some cash. Cockatiels are very prolific, and may produce up to four clutches a year. This means that they are very common, and therefore do not command top dollar. Factor in the expenses of more food and additional cages—not to mention the amount of time you'll have to invest in socializing the chicks so that they'll be tame when it's time to sell them—and any profit that you might make diminishes rapidly.

All of this aside, if you have a bird or birds that are determined to lay eggs, there is not an awful lot you can do to stop them. This chapter will

Cockatiel fathers are devoted and involved parents, taking their turn sitting on the nest and feeding the chicks.

help guide you through the prospect of mating, nesting, eggs, and possibly even chicks.

The Mating Mood

If you watch your cockatiel carefully, you'll begin to notice signs that the bird is starting to have thoughts of nesting. Beginning as early as 10 months to a year old, you'll notice birds of either sex start to take an interest in exploring dark, enclosed spaces. Open cabinets, the space under your dresser, and open boxes all create great interest and excitement. If you have more than one bird, the finder of a potential nest will call to its mate and stand nervously by as the discovery is inspected. If the bird thinks it's found an acceptable nest, it will whistle and strut and generally seem quite pleased with itself. Otherwise, it will keep on looking.

When the birds are getting ready to mate, there will be an extensive courtship involving whistling, feeding, and preening each other, and general attentiveness. When the female is ready, she will assume a crouched position, with her body parallel to the floor, her head lowered, her crest down, and her tail raised. It is not unheard of for a hen to assume this position for her human companion even though, of course, there is no hope of consummation. Similarly, you may suddenly realize that your male cockatiel is courting you, possibly even going as far as to rub himself against you in a sexual manner. Males are also known to masturbate with a favorite toy or on a convenient

Baby normal gray being hand-fed.

perch if they are unable to find any relief in the traditional manner.

When it's time to mate, the male will carefully climb onto the female's back and rub his vent area against hers, tail swishing madly as he struggles to keep his balance and accommodate her at the same time. Some birds are particularly noisy while mating—you may want to move the cage to a distant part of the house if you are planning to entertain during one of the cockatiels' amorous periods. Otherwise, you may find yourself hastily throwing a towel over the cage while your birds have noisy, joyful relations in front of the visiting parish priest (trust me—it happened!). Cockatiels have no inhibitions when it comes to procreating with an audience present.

If you decide that you do want to let your cockatiels reproduce, provide them with a nest box filled with wood shavings. The box can be made of wood or cardboard, with a hole cut out as a door. A cockatiel nest box should be at least 9 by 12 inches (22.5 by 30 cm). Cockatiels will normally chew on the entrance to the nest box, enlarging it to their liking, and may toss out the wood shavings that they don't find up to snuff.

Not all males are particularly adept at their first attempts at mating, and the females, in frustration, may nip at them. This is normal. Sometimes mating is as much trial and error as instinct, but they all seem to figure it out in the end. If mating is successful, the first egg should appear anywhere from one to three weeks later.

Eggs

One of the most obvious signs that a hen is getting ready to lay an egg is that her droppings occur less frequently, and when she does poop, the amount of droppings is positively huge and the consistency is very loose and liquid. This is because the hen doesn't want to defecate near the place where she plans to lay her eggs, both for hygienic reasons and because she doesn't want to leave a clue to predators that there's a nesting bird nearby. She will "hold it" until she gets an opportunity to relieve herself away from her cage and nest, or until she literally can't wait any longer. The resulting deluge can be as much as two tablespoons or more.

If you have a hen in this condition, take care not to hold her on your shoulder or over your clothing until she's relieved herself. In fact, after you first start to notice that her droppings have been unusually large, you might want to hold her over a wastebasket as soon as you take her out of the cage. These hens usually relieve themselves within minutes of getting out of the cage, and it's much easier to hold her over a lined wastebasket than it is to clean up the mess from your clothing, furniture, rug, and the like.

Some cockatiels will mate and lay whether or not they have a potential nest site. These females will lay their eggs on the cage floor, on top of your bookshelf, or even in your hand. The first egg is generally not sat upon until the second egg is laid, but sometimes just a single egg is laid and that's the end of it. No more eggs follow and the hen ignores her egg. More often, though, multiple eggs are laid and the hen will sit on them wherever they happen to be. Whether or not these eggs hatch depends on whether or not a male bird fertilized them. If the hen who laid them is an only bird, or if all of the cockatiels in the house are female and there has been no access to a male cockatiel for the past month, the eggs will be infertile and will not hatch, although the mother bird may still go through all the motions of incubating them.

If you have a hen that lays unwanted eggs, the best course of action is to let her sit on them. She'll continue to do this diligently for several weeks before she finally decides that they aren't going to hatch and gives up. Remember, she will not be her usual sweet self while she's sitting (although she may be willing to spend time with you if you can get her away from the cage and eggs). If you remove the eggs, she will simply lay replacements. This constant laying of replacement eggs will put a tremendous strain on her as she uses up her body's store of nutrients to form the eggs. It's healthier for her if you simply let her follow her instincts and sit on them until she gets tired of it and gives up.

If you have eggs that you suspect may be fertile, and you definitely do not want chicks, remove the eggs one at a time as they are laid and simply stick them in the refrigerator for a day or two before replacing them in the nest. The prolonged exposure to the cool temperature should be enough to stop the embryo from developing. After about a week, you can tell if an egg is fertile or not by "candling" it, or holding it up to a source of light. Special lights are available at some pet supply stores, but holding it up to a strong flashlight, or even close to a regular house lightbulb will also allow you to see if the egg is opaque or not. If you're not sure, hold up the first egg laid and the most recent one. If there are chicks growing inside, you can see the difference. Light won't shine through the shell the same way if there's a chick inside, and you should be able to make out the air sack at one end where light does get through if the egg is fertile.

It's normal for the parents to ignore the first egg that is laid for a day or two. Once they start laying, the eggs will generally arrive one every other day. Baby cockatiels hatch after approximately 18 to 21 days of incubation. This is counted not from the day the eggs are laid, but from the day the parents begin to sit on them. It's not unusual for a pair of cockatiels to lay an egg and then seem to ignore it. They frequently delay sitting until there are two eggs, increasing the odds that the eggs will hatch on or about the same day. Thus, the first two chicks start out on more or less equal footing as they compete to be fed. Subsequent chicks will be smaller than their older siblings, and each successive chick will find it harder and harder to compete for the food their parents bring.

Egg Binding

One of the most heartbreaking causes of death in female cockatiels is egg binding, when the hen is literally unable to pass an egg out of its body, struggling to expel the egg until she dies. The cause can be poor nutrition, an exceptionally large egg, or a hen whose pelvis is uncommonly small.

Signs of an egg-bound hen include a bird that is crouched on the floor of the cage or the nest box, visibly straining. She may sit with her eyes closed, feathers ruffled, and tail bobbing or wagging, and her breath-

ing may be labored. She may sit on her tail feathers with her legs spread apart in an effort to get the egg to pass, and you may notice a large bulge where the egg sits inside her abdomen. Her legs and feet may turn bluish-white if the position of the egg interferes with the flow of blood to the extremities.

Hens normally pass their eggs fairly easily and fairly quickly. If you notice a cockatiel hen that appears to be trying to pass an egg and this goes on for close to an hour, assume that the hen is egg bound and that this is a life-threatening emergency. Left untreated, she will go into shock and die.

Get her to a veterinarian as soon as you possibly can. The longer you delay, the less likely your bird is to survive. Do not attempt to break the shell of the egg inside her on the theory that this will make it smaller and easier to pass; not only will it not help, it increases the risk of infection or that the broken bits of shell will puncture her internally, creating a whole new set of potentially fatal complications.

If a delay in getting the cockatiel to a veterinarian is unavoidable, there are some steps you can take to help ease her struggles and to ward off the onset of shock. Gently move the bird to your hospital cage, and place the cage on an electric blanket or heating pad set so that the temperature inside the cage is between 85 and 90°F (29-32°C). You can try to ease the passage of the egg by gently rubbing vegetable oil, mineral oil, or petroleum jelly around her cloaca and on the visible part of the egg to lubricate things a bit. Then take her into the bathroom and run the water in the shower as hot as you can, making the bathroom steamy so that the heat and humidity will help her muscles to relax. (Note: You're not putting the bird in the shower or getting her wet, you're just creating a steam room for her.) Even if she successfully manages to pass the egg, you'll still want to get her to the veterinarian as soon as possible, since there will likely be another egg and a possible repeat of the emergency in another 48 hours.

Chicks

Cockatiel chicks hatch in the order in which their eggs were laid, after 18 to 21 days of incubation. You can actually hear the chicks peeping inside the shell during the last few days of incubation if you hold the egg up to your ear—a sign that it will hatch within the next 48 hours or so.

There's a good chance that you'll notice the chick starting to break out of the egg before it actually makes it out. Breaking through the shell is a tough job and may take a day or two. Don't be tempted to help things along by removing the chick from the egg once you see it starting to hatch. It will still have some of the yolk sac attached, and pulling the

shell away could also pull away the yolk sac, with potentially fatal results. If the chick starts to get distressed, the parents can help it out of the shell if needed.

Baby cockatiels are really ugly, with bald heads that seem to be taken up almost entirely by closed, bulbous eyes, no ear openings, yellow or white fluff over most of their bodies, and tiny little feet and wings. The fluff is wet when the chick first hatches, but it quickly dries. Their heads seem almost too big for their bodies, and holding them up seems to take a huge effort. The babies will frequently rest with their heads propped up on the unhatched eggs or on each other. Doing this not only helps to keep them warm, but helps to incubate the other eggs and chicks with their body heat. You can see through the membrane covering the eyes if the eyes are red or black—your first indication of what mutation the chick will be when it gets its feathers in.

It may be several hours before the parent feeds the chick, and you might be quite alarmed the first time you see it. It looks like the parent is trying to kill the baby. It covers the chick's beak with its own and bobs its head up and down almost violently, while the chick makes a loud *peep*! at each shake. Don't panic— the bobbing motion is necessary for the parent to regurgitate food into the baby's mouth. You should be able to hear the process every time the chicks are fed, even if you don't look inside the nest box.

Eyes open and feathers begin to appear about ten days after hatching. Note the bulging crop on the throat of both birds.

There is a myth that if people touch a baby bird, the parents will detect the scent of humans on the chick and abandon it. This isn't true, either with wild birds or with cockatiels. You can pick the babies up to examine them if you can get past the parents. You may notice a large "sack" at the base of the throat that seems to be considerably bigger after the baby's been fed. This is the crop. Sometimes you can even see the food in the crop through the skin after the feeding, an indication that the parents are doing an excellent job taking care of the baby. A full crop can look almost alarmingly large—a third-grade student of mine once looked at the crop, blinked, and exclaimed, "Whoa! That thing's gonna need a

bra to hold that up!" In fact, the food is absorbed and digested quite quickly, and the parents will soon be hard pressed to keep all of the little crops filled.

After the first two eggs hatch, the rest of the clutch should hatch one every 48 hours or so, although once in a while you'll get one that hatches a few days sooner or takes a few days longer. The chicks will grow at an astonishing rate; you may even notice a size difference between the morning and the night. Because of this, the older chicks will be markedly bigger than their younger siblings, and it's not uncommon for the smallest chicks to be unable to compete for their parents' attention at feeding time, and consequently starve to death.

Hand-Feeding

If the parents do not feed the chicks, or if you want to hand-feed one or more of the older chicks to give the youngest ones a better chance of surviving, you can take over, but be warned: Hand-feeding very small chicks is a delicate proposition, and a lot of things can go wrong. Packages of hand-feeding formula for exotic birds are sold at pet stores, as are syringes. (The syringes at my local pet store are too big for tiny cockatiel beaks, so I use a medicine dispenser designed for a human infant or a plastic spoon that's been dipped into boiling water and pinched to act more like a funnel.) Instructions for how to mix the formula are found on the package—

it needs to be different consistencies for babies of different ages. Pay careful attention to the temperature; you can actually burn a hole through the baby's crop if the formula is too hot. I like to double-check the thermometer by squirting a little of the formula on the inside of my wrist, as I would a baby bottle, to make sure that it's warm, but not too hot.

Feed the baby chick using the same technique you would to medicate an adult (see page 112), squirting the formula in from the right side to the left a little at a time. You'll be able to see the formula collecting in the crop. Stop when you have a comfortable-sized bulge (a new cockatiel will only hold a couple of milliliters of formula). If you give it

too much, you risk getting formula into the lungs, which will be fatal. It's better to give smaller, more frequent feedings than to risk that. A newly hatched cockatiel will require feeding every two hours around the clock, with feedings becoming less frequent as the baby grows.

You can handle babies to socialize them, without actually hand-feeding, and end up with a pet that's just as happy and confident as one that was raised entirely by people. In my house, we begin handling them soon after their eyes are open, and my kids will sit and watch TV holding onto a baby, rubbing its face, and talking to it. Just make sure that the baby stays warm, preferably by holding it near your body.

Cockatiel Development

Baby cockatiels develop very quickly. The eyes and ears start to open at the end of the first week. Shadows of incoming feather sheaths are visible around day 10, and in the next few days there is a resemblance to a baby porcupine. By three weeks of age, most of the down is gone, although the belly and back are still bare. A few days later, the feather sheaths start to open, tips first, so that the baby begins to look like an exploded pincushion. By four weeks, the feathers are in although the tail is still short, and small, curious faces begin to appear at the opening to the nest box. It's now just a matter of time before the chicks venture out to explore the

world on their own. By six weeks, they may be sampling real food and begin flapping their wings in anticipation of flight. Weaning should occur around eight weeks, more or less, and the babies should be ready to go to their new homes shortly thereafter.

Once the babies are out of the nest box, immediately remove it. If you used a cardboard box, throw it away; if you used a wooden box, clean it thoroughly and put it away. If you leave the box, the parents will want to do it all over again. For the sake of the hen, a pair of cockatiels should not be allowed to produce more than two clutches a year.

Resources

Magazines
Bird Talk
P.O. Box 6050
Mission Viejo, CA 92690-6050
www.birdchannel.com

Bird Times
Pet Publishing, Inc.
4642 West Market Street, #368
Greensboro, NC 27407
www.petpublishing.com/birdtimes

Parrots Magazine
P.O. Box 386
Goleta, CA 93116-0386
www.parrotmag.com

Books
Athan, Mattie Sue. *Guide to a Well-Behaved Parrot*. Hauppauge, NY: Barron's Educational Series, Inc., 1999.
Athan, Mattie Sue and Dianalee Deter. *The Second-Hand Parrot*. Hauppauge, NY: Barron's Educational Series, Inc., 2005.
Grindol, Diane. *The Complete Book of Cockatiels*. New York: Howell Book House, 1998.

Higdon, Pamela. *The Essential Cockatiel*. New York: Howell Book House, 1999.
Moustaki, Nikki. *Why Do Cockatiels Do That? Real Answers to the Curious Things Cockatiels Do*. Mission Viejo, CA: BowTie Press, 2003.

Cockatiel Organizations
National Cockatiel Society
www.cockatiels.org

American Cockatiel Society
www.acstiels.com

Helpful Web Sites
American Society for the Prevention of Cruelty to Animals (ASPCA)
www.aspca.org

Association of Avian Veterinarians
www.aav.org

Petfinder.com
www.petfinder.com

Index

A

age, 43–44
alcohol, 102, 111
allergies, 8
aspergillosis, 117
avocados, 97, 102

B

bathing, 67–69
beaks, 69, 92, 93
bedding, 29–30
behavior, 52, 77–93
    see also personality
Birdie Bread, 99
biting, 78–80
bleeding, 121
body language, 88–93
books, 137
bowing, 89–90
breeding, 2, 38, 126–132
burns, 121

C

caffeine, 102
cages, 7, 14, 19–23, 55–56,
    122–123
calcium, 27, 101–102
carriers, 32
cat bites, 121
cats and cockatiels, 11
cereals, 95
chemicals and cleaning
    products, 111–112
chicks, 132–136
children and cockatiels, 9, 11
chocolate, 102
cinnamon cockatiels, 50
classification, 3
cleaning products, 111–112

coloration, 2, 45–52
convulsions, 121
cost of ownership, 13
crests, 89
crouching, 90–91
cuttlebones, 27–28

D

dairy products, 101–102
dander, 7–8
dehydration, 121, 124
diarrhea, 124
diet, 31–32, 71–72, 94–102
disabled birds, 41
discipline, 78
dishes, 28–29
dogs and cockatiels, 11
droppings, 53–54

E

egg binding, 130–132
eggs and egg laying, 90–91,
    101–102, 129–132
electrical wires, 111
eye problems, 124

F

fallow cockatiels, 50–51
fats, 102
feathers, 52–53, 63–67, 82–86
first aid, 113, 120–121,
    124–125
food and feeding, 31–32,
    71–72, 94–102
fruits and vegetables, 97–100

G

gender, 42–43
giardiasis, 117

grains, 95
gram stain test, 116

H

hand-fed cockatiels, 44–45
hand-feeding, 134–135
handling, 59–60, 69–73
head rubbing, 62
heat and eat mixes,
    100–101
heatstroke, 124
history and background
    information, 1–4
hospital cages, 122–123

I

illness checklist, 119
illnesses, 33–34, 52–54,
    83–84, 115–125
incubation period, 132
introductions, 56–59
isolation cages, 122–123

J

jewelry, 15

L

leg bands, 104
light requirements, 21–22
longevity, 7
lost birds, 103–104, 106
lutinos, 46–47

M

magazines, 137
masturbation, 91
mating, 127–129
medications, 112–114
messiness, 7–8

metals, toxic, 106–107
microchips, 104, 106
mineral blocks, 27–28
mites, 36, 83–84
molting, 83
moths, 96
mutations, 45–52

N
nail clipping, 67
name, scientific, 3–4
nests and nesting, 127–129,
    136
nibbling, 15, 78–79
night frights, 86
nonstick cookware, 110–111
normal gray cockatiels,
    45–46
nutrition, 31–32, 71–72,
    94–102
nymphicus hollandicus, 3–4

O
organizations, 137
other birds, 11–12, 56–59
out-of-cage time, 14–15
ownership pros and cons, 10,
    13–18

P
Pacheco's disease, 117–118
parent-fed cockatiels, 44–45,
    132–133
PDD (proventricular dilation
    disease), 119–120
pearl cockatiels, 47–48
pellets, 96–97
perches, 24–27, 36
personality, 4–6
pet stores, 39
pied cockatiels, 48, 50
plants, poisonous, 107–110
play stands, 23–24

plucking, 82–86
poisoning, 124–125
    see also poisonous plants;
    toxic metals
poisonous plants, 107–110
polyoma, 118–119
polytetrafluoroethylene
    (PTFE), 110–111
potty training, 73–75
preening, 15, 60–61
proventricular dilation
    disease (PDD), 119–120
psittacosis, 120
PTFE
    (polytetrafluoroethylene),
    110–111
purchasing, 37–54

Q
quarantine, 55

R
re-homing, 16–17
reproduction, 126–132
resources, 137
routine care, 63–69

S
salt, 102
scientific name, 3–4
screaming, 80–82
secondhand birds, 39–40
seeds, 94–95
sexual readiness, 90–91,
    127–129
shaking, 93
shedding, 7–8
shipping, 32–33
shock, 125
shoulder sitting, 59–60, 62
silver cockatiels, 51
size, 3, 6–7
sneezing, 54

socializing, 14–15
split cockatiels, 51–52
standing on one foot, 92–93
standing tall and thin, 91–92
stepping up, 59, 73
stress, 84–85
supply list, 28

T
tail rubbing, 91
talking, 9, 75–76
taming, 6, 69–73
temperature requirements, 7,
    21–22
territorialism, 86–88
time requirements, 14
toxic metals, 106–107
toxic plants, 107–110
toys, 30–31
treats, 101
tricks, 73–76

V
vegetables and fruits,
    97–100
veterinarians, 34–35
vitamins, 36, 100
vocalization, 8–9, 42, 75–76,
    80–82
vomiting, 125

W
water bottles, 28–29
water hazards, 11
weight and weighing, 33–34,
    115–116
whistling, 9, 76
whiteface cockatiels, 51
wing clipping, 63–67, 103

Y
yawning, 93
yellowface cockatiels, 51